WHAT MATTERS

MOST

Also by Keisha Watson

A Cry For Help

And

Pain Wrong Turn

Copyright 2009 by Keisha Watson
ISBN 978-0-557-23700-5

All right reserved. No part of this book may be reproduced, stored or transmitted by any means—whether auditory, graphic, mechanical or electronic—without permission of both the publishers and author, except in the case of brief excerpts used in critical articles and reviews. Unauthorized reproduction of any part of this work is illegal and is punishable by law.

WHAT MATTERs
MOsT

A Novel

Keisha Ann Watson

CHAPTER ONE

Paper chaser.
    " Nigga, run me my money homie!" Shyann said.
    " Aww, come on Shyann you know I'm good for it." Black said.
    " Nigga, give me my money first or I'm out!"
    " Alright, alright damn. How much, 300 right?"
    " Black, why you trying to play me, run me 350$ or I'm out homie."
    " Damn, a nigga can't get a discount we do this every week."
    " Hell naw, I eat at the Taco Shack every week too and they don't show me no love, so I ain't showing yo grimy ass no love." He handed Shyann 360$.
    " I ain't got no change."
    " Don't trip, I'll through in a little extra. Undress."

    Shyann was all about her paper and wasn't going to let no one get over her. She was a real hustler and did what she had to, to support her two kids.

    " You know the rules, and let's not forget you got 30 minutes." Shyann said.
    " Shut up and come ride this dick girl." Black said.

Shyann was a fly ass chick, niggas would do whatever she wanted them to do. She had it all, from the looks to the books, and street smarts out this world. One time she made this one nigga drop a g on her just from a conversation. That nigga nutted on himself like three times. She whispered some shit in his ear and gave him a lap dance out of this world.

" Black, you got five minutes left." Shyann said.
" Damn baby, you do this all the time, sometimes I be wishing you forget and we make love all night." Black said, as he began to pump harder to cum.
" Nigga please, making love? I don't love you and you fo' damn show don't love me. I'm about my paper, you know that! So hurry up, now you got three minutes.
" Awww, shit. I'm about to cum." Black screamed pushing Shyann off him and doubling over in the bed shaking. Shyann just looked and began getting dressed, and cell phone rings.

" Hey baby."
" Mama, Mercedes didn't pick me up from School and it's almost 5." Lexus said crying.
" Ok, baby mommy is on the way. I love you and see you in a few minutes."
" Ok, love you too mama."
" Black, I got to go. Same time next week?"
" Man yeah, and wear something sexy."
" Shut up, I'm always sexy. I'll holla."

Shyann grabbed her keys and left to pick up Lexus from School. The whole ride she was thinking to herself, what she was going to do to Mercedes. Mercedes is 15 years old and everyday after School she knows she's suppose to get Lexus at 4:30 and go straight home. Lexus is 7, their father is in jail so Shyann is trying her hardest to raise them alone. Shyann pulls into the School parking lot and Lexus is sitting on the front steps.

" Mama!" Lexus saw Shyann walking up and ran to her.
" Hi baby. You hungry?" Lexus shook her head yes. " Come on baby, let's go."

Shyann and Lexus drove home. They stayed in a nice three bedroom, two bath house with a huge backyard. Shyann took a quick shower and began to cook dinner. Lexus went in her room to do her homework. About 6 o'clock Mercedes walks in the house.

" Mercedes get your ass in here." Shyann yelled.
" What's up ma?" Mercedes said as if she wasn't suppose to pick up Lexus.
" Whats up ma? Girl who you talking to like that? I call you answer yes. Do you understand?"
" Yes mother!" She said rolling her eyes.
" Okay, so you forgot about your sister or what?"
" Ah shit!"
Shyann looked at her in shock. Before she knew what she had done she had Mercedes by the collar and backed up in the corner.
" Who do you think you talking to? I ain't them little girls at School you think you be bulling. I would wipe you little ass clean."
" Sorry mama, it slipped and won't happen again. We had a science project and my group all went to Tyler's house to work on it."
" Didn't I tell you I didn't want you on that side of l.a.? You think you just so damn grown huh? Keep on, you must not want to live to see 18. Next time, wait you know what, there isn't going to be a next time right?"
" No mama."
" Yall got a project to do, work on it here. If I have to stop what I'm doing to go get Lexus again were going to box. Got that?" They both shared a smile.
" Now go apologize to your sister and do your homework if it isn't done and if so help your sister with hers."
" Ok ma."
" Hey, I love you!"
" Love you too mother." Mercedes said with a smile on her face.

" Hey!"

" I'm mad at you. You left me and the other kids were picking on me." Lexus said as her eyes filled with tears.

" I am so sorry. I promise it'll never happen again."

" Pinky swear?"

" Pinky swear!" Mercedes gave her little sister a hug. " Who picking on you?"

" The fourth and fifth graders."

" Okay, don't trip. Tomorrow I'm going to pick you up earlier and I want you to piont them out to me, ok?"

" Ok." Lexus said then put her head down.

" Don't worry about them, big sis has your back."

Shyann loved her daughters very much and always taught them to stick by each other side no matter what. Shyann had Mercedes at 16 and Nate (which is their father) was 20. Nate was a drug dealer and is currently in jail for murder. He went to jail about a month after Lexus first birthday. He had about 20,000 stashed away in their apartment they were staying in, in east l.a., Shyann snatched it up and took the kids and left. Nate was loaded with paper, when people found out he was going to prison for murder, they did that nigga dirty as hell. He had 2 mill and 25 kilos at the spot where they served and all that shit was gone. Nate found out his so-called crew did him dirty and told Shyann to take the kids and shake.

Shyann is very smart she got her masters in Business Management and Nate put her up on so much game about the streets. She's one smart ass chick. Her and the kids have never been without and she always said the niggas that took from her kids are going to pay. Shyann is very beautiful with long dark hair. Body of gold, I mean perfect! She's 5'6" nicely built, ass for days, chest for days and you'd never think she was 31 with two kids. All the men want her, but she's all about her daughters and her paper so she doesn't give them any play.

" Dinners ready girls!" Shyann yelled for the girls to come eat dinner.
" Ok coming." The girls replied.

They sat as a family and ate dinner, something Shyann tried her hardest to do every night before she goes to work. They ate dinner and Mercedes cleaned the kitchen while Shyann got ready for work and checked Lexus homework. She's scheduled for work at 8pm, (even though she makes up her own schedule and does what she wants), she gets away with it because she's the baddiest bitch in there and most of the customers are there to see her. The girls in the club don't like her at all, but they respect her to the fullest. She's the best dancer at Tasty's and indeed the hottest.

" Ok mommy has to go to work, I want you to listen to your sister. Take a shower and go to bed, ok Lexie?" Shyann kissed her and gave her a hug.
" Ok mama." Lexus said and went into the bathroom to take a shower.
" Love you, I'll be home soon. Set the alarm soon as I close the door. Mercedes don't be on the phone all night either. Call me if you need me."
" Ok. ma! Same speech every night." She said with a smile.
" Good, so you can never say you didn't hear me." Shyann gave Mercedes a kiss and left.
" Love you." Mercedes yelled from the front door. Shyann blew a kiss and hopped in her Range Rover and left.

Mercedes was a good big sister, she looked out for Lexus as if that was her child.
" Lexus, you ok in there?"
" Yes, I'll be out in a few minutes." Lexus yelled through the door.
" Ok, bed by 9 missy, don't forget."
" Okay."

Mercedes did just what her mother asked her not to do, be on the phone all night. Mercedes was a little fast, she started her period about six months ago. She's beautiful just like her mom. She has a little nice size butt and her chest are pretty big for her height, she's 5'2" with cup sizes 32C's, she's very thin. Shyann let her try out for cheer leading and Mercedes made Varsity. She's in the 10th grade, some guy on the football team got her head over hills sprung. He's in the 11th grade and his name is Chris Malton. They talk for hours on the phone every night.

" I miss you too." Mercedes responded to Chris.
" You should invite me over, so we can. . . you know?" Chris said smiling through the phone.
" Hell, naw! My mom will kill me, plus I set the alarm and we have the one where you can check the last time it was disarmed."
" So there's no way we can be together tonight?"
" Uh... no." Mercedes fakes a yarn. "I'm sleepy, see you tomorrow." She hangs up the phone.

Mercedes was sprung when it came to Chris but was far from dumb. She went to check on Lexus. She lay sound asleep peacefully. Mercedes turned off the television and put the covers over her and cracked the door. Then she took a shower and went to bed.

CHAPTER TWO

Always talking shit!

" You're late!" Ben said, the club manager.

" Ben, please you know I got kids." Shyann said. "Star up in 10 DJ." She turned to the DJ and said.

" Gotcha!" Grabs the mic. " Alright, we got Star on deck next. Now were enjoying lovely Peaches, Come'on show her some love fellas."

Shyann walks in the locker room and everyone speaks. " Hey ladies." She gets dressed and heads to the bar and orders a shot of patron.

" Thanks baby, he's going to pay for it right here." She told Lace the bartender, pointing to a guy sitting at the bar. " Hey baby, you got this drink for me?" She asked.

" Yes, baby. They way you look you can order whatever you like." The guy said smiling and handing Lace a 20$ bill.

" Thanks babe!" Kisses him on the cheek and walks away, as the DJ calls for Star to the stage.

Star pulled her hair up into a high ponytail that stopped in the middle of her back. She had on a black bikini top with a black g-string. Her heels were about 4 inches high, she stood tall and breath taking. Ass completely out and her breasts were big and juicy, 34DD's. Every time she got on stage she made no less than 300$. She danced and moved her body in ways that would cause you to cum instantly. Star had money flying all over the stage and all the men surrounded her and praised her. The other girls in the club was jealous and couldn't stand her, but they respected her.

Star danced for three songs, the crowd screamed for more. Star! Star! Star! The next dancer to come behind her was afraid because she knew she had to bring it just the same or better. Star gathered her money and went off stage to the little holding room and counted it. Star counted 569$. Three 100$ bills, all with Mike and his phone number on them. She didn't recall meeting a Mike but made a note to find out who he was and see how much more he was trying to spend.

Star walked pass the stage while a dancer Tiny was dancing and noticed it was only a few dollars up there. Star threw 40$ in ones on the stage for her. Tiny looked at her with such a hateful look and rolled her eyes. Star didn't pay that broke bitch no mind and continued doing her. She yelled to Lace. " Ma, Let me get a double please."
" I gotcha. Who got the ticket?"
" I do." The same guy that paid for Star's first shot replied. He looked at Star and smiled. Star walked over to him.
" I ain't seen you around here. Let me guess, Mike?" Star said as she took the stool next to him.
" Yup. You are so sexy."
" Thanks babe. So, what's up? How can Star be at service?" Lace gave her the double and Star took it straight to the head in one gulp. He leaned over and whispered into her ear.
" How's your head game?"
" I ain't got no head game baby, I kiss my kids with these lips."
" Oh, you got kids with that body?"
" Sure do, so what else can I help you with, because I got money to rack up baby." He handed her two 100$ bills.
" How much time does that buy for a conversations?" Mike said with a grin on his face.
" I got a few regulars waiting for me but they can wait a little while I guess. You want a lap dance babe?"
" Sure, why not." Star grabbed him by the hand and led him into the lap dancing area to an empty cubical.

Star began dancing in front of him and he grabbed her to sit on his lap. She hopped up and stood in front of him and grabbed him by the neck.

" I have a problem with people touching me without asking." She let his neck go and looked him in the eyes. "I dance my way or no way at all." Star made so much money because she knew how to tease the fellas and make them want it more and more. She would dance with a nigga for 20 songs straight and make that nigga feel like he hit.

" Okay, see that's why I like you. I love a woman who takes control and does what she wants. I respect that. How much you charge?"

" Charge for what?"

" I want to make love to you."

" Make love, to make love you have to be in love. You want to fuck. Because that's all it'll be babe, don't fall in love."

" How much?"

Star wasn't a fool, she could tell this nigga had paper. He looked about 35-40. He was very handsome Carmel soft skin and didn't have a lot of facial hair so that made him look younger. He was dressed in a suit and smelled nice. Star thought he was kind of cute, but always kept business, business.

" 500$."

" 500 all night, that's not bad."

" All night my ass, 5 for every 30." Star said with her hands on her hips.

" Okay, that ain't shit. Can we do it here?"

" Nigga, hell naw. I don't fuck at work. I either come to your house or you get a room. Your choice babe."

" Ok, you can come to my house. I want an hour." Mike said.

" Ok, that's no problem. I got a few rules though. As you know the first one already, don't touch me unless you ask. You also know the second one I don't give head. I don't cuddle afterwards. Run me my money before we start. No hitting and telling. I'm strictly about my paper so when your time is up I will be letting you know. We ain't making love so don't be sucking all over my neck leaving marks and shit. And last but not least, wrap yo' shit up. Got it?"

" Dang ma, is that it? You killing me."

" For now that's it, if I feel like adding more, I will."

" Alright, my number on them bills. Call me tomorrow." Mike gets up to walk out the cubical and Star stands in front of him. " Now what ma?"

" Nigga, we were in here talking for four songs, 20 bucks each. You owe me 80$ baby."

" Ah, ma I just gave you 200$ before went came in at the bar."
" Exactly, before when we were at the bar, not for the dance's! I don't care you owe me for these songs."
" Ma, you are something else." He handed Star another 100$ bill. Star checked it to see if it was real, then told him thanks.
" Man, you sexy as fuck. I can't wait to hit that!" Mike walked out.

Star made her rounds with her customers and went home with 1,700$ after pay out. Stacy, which is the only girl Shyann really talks to in the club, asked Star for a ride and had their usual conversation.

" How much you rack up ma?" Star said.
" Man tonight I did bad, I got like 500 after pay out. I know yo' ass did good as usual."
" You got to be in control, they'll walk over the weak hoes and play'em. I'm not saying you're weak but you just need to be Schooled." Stacy just started working there about four months ago and was new to this whole lifestyle. Shyann took her under her wings because she saw she was different and didn't want the other girls to turn her out.
" I know."
" 5 ain't bad though, you made that in one night, don't beat yourself up. I gotcha. I'll teach you some tricks."
" Right here." Pointing to the apartment building. "Thanks girl, I see why you're the best."
" You got my number, hit me up. I'll School you. When I get some shit lined up and I need another female I'm going to keep you in mind. If you want these niggas paper, fuck with me. Alright, have a good night girl."
" Ok, thanks." Stacy said and hopped out the Range and Shyann drove off.

Shyann been there, Stacy young so Shyann told herself she'll look after her. Shyann got in the house, checked on the girls and took a shower and went to bed.

CHAPTER THREE

Same routine.

Every morning Shyann wakes up at 6:30 am no matter how late she got in the house, she keeps her kids first. She fixes them breakfast and packs Lexus lunch and help her get dressed for School. She drops Lexus off first then Mercedes.

" Hey, baby have a good day at School. I love you."

" I love you too mama." Lexus kisses her mom and Mercedes on the cheek from the backseat and gets out the truck.

" Later." Mercedes says.

" Don't forget her today or I'm going to kick your ass."

" Ok, ma I wont."

Mercedes School was a few blocks from Lexus. So Mercedes didn't have to travel far to pick her up. Shyann pulled up in front of Mercedes School and gave her a kiss on the cheek.

" Thanks mama. Love you."

" Love you too." Shyann said as Mercedes was already half way out the truck.

It was 8am and Shyann needed to catch up on rest. She sleeps for four hours every day after she drops off the girls. She got up at noon and cleaned the house up and washed the kids clothes. She went into Mercedes rooms to put away her clothes. She walked toward the door and saw a note on her desk. It was from Chris.

Hey boo,

You looked cute today in those tight ass apple bottom jeans. I got hard just looking at you. So what's up? You know I love you, you love me? Let's take it to the next level Cedes. I mean why wait we love each other. Let me know when you're ready. I'm waiting on you.

Love, big daddy Chris

This little girl better not be thinking about having sex, Shyann thought to herself. Maybe it's time to have a sex talk with Mercedes. She just wants the best for her kids and wants them to wait til marriage or at least to a descent age. Shyann put the letter back how she found it and finished the laundry. It was about 3:00 pm and she gave Mike a call.

" Hey, it's Star."
" What's up ma, you ready to do this?"
" I'm always ready to make money. What's up, where you want me to meet you at?"
" Can we meet at 5:30?"
" We can do that babe, no problem. Run me the address, I'm about to grab a pen."
" Ready?"
" Yup, shoot."
" 9291 3rd Ave off Main. Need directions?"
" Nope, I'm a big girl I know l.a. very well."
" Alright, bring that sexy ass attitude too, that shit turn me on."
" Later." Shyann hung up the phone.

She wanted to get the girls some clothes and shoes so she went to the Beverly Center to shop. Every time she hit the streets eyes paused. Shyann was hot. She valet parked and went straight to the kids favorite store H&M for some clothes. She picked out 3 outfits for both of the girls the headed to Footlocker to get them some kicks. She got them 2 pairs of shoes each. She usually stops by the Coach store and grabs whatever they have new and hot, but she knew she had money to make so ran in and ran out.

Mercedes picked up Lexus at 4:00 and told her to point out the kids that were picking on here. Lexus did it.
" Aye!" Mercedes screamed for them to turn around. " Yeah yall." As they just looked at Mercedes walked toward them.
" Which one of yall being messing with my sister?" None of

the kids said anything. " I'm going to ask one more time. Which one of yall been messing with my sister?" No one replied so Mercedes slapped all three of the kids in the face one by one really fast. "Fuck with her again and watch what I'll do to yall next time." Mercedes grabbed Lexus and walked away. Lexus turned to look back at them, stuck out her tongue and smile.

" Thanks Cedes."

" If they mess with you again, let me know. Let's go home."

" Okay."

They went home and didn't see their moms truck. So Mercedes knew she had to look after her sister til Shyann got home.

" Go do your homework Lexus."

" Ok."

About 20 minutes passed and Shyann walks in the house and Lexus hops up to meet her at the door. " Hi mama." Lexus said smiling.

" Hi, baby. How was School?" Shyann said handing her some bags. "I got you something, where's Cedes?"

" I'm right here. Hey mama." Mercedes said walking down the hallway.

" School was good. H&M bags, yes!" Lexus said very excited.

" What you get me?" Cedes said.

" Come look, a few outfits and a pair of jordans and some blazers. They were too cute." Shyann replied.

" Hey, how would you guys feel about pizza tonight?"

" Sounds goo to me! How about you Mercedes?" Lexus said trying on her new shoes.

" That's fine. I'll order it."

" Ok. I'm going to take a shower I have to be somewhere at 5:30." Shyann went into her bathroom and took a long hot shower and got dressed. When she came out the pizza man was just leaving. "Wow, they delivered fast today."

" Yeah they got this new thing, they have to deliver in 30 minutes or less." Mercedes said.

Shyann wasn't really hungry but she wanted to sit down with the girls and eat something with them. She took a few bites and couldn't eat the rest.

" I'll be back in about an hour or so."

" Okay mama, love you." Mercedes said.

" Set the alarm."

" Mama, I know, we go through this every time you leave. I'll help Lexus with her homework and make sure she showers as well. I got it mama, see you later." Mercedes smiled.

Shyann just smiled and walked away. She noticed something was wrong with Mercedes and told herself she'll talk to her when she came back home. Shyann drove to Mike's place, she's very familiar with Los Angeles so she got there in no time. She pulled up at about 5:20 parked and walked up to the door. Shyann was a very tuff cat, she'll pop a nigga so fast and sleep peaceful at night. She always kept her pistol on her, either her 45, 9 or 38. She rang the doorbell and a few seconds later Mike opened the door wearing a cream colored robe.

" Wow, you look ready." Shyann said as she walked in the house. Mike had the living room over flowing with candles he lit and rose petals. He prepared a little area with blankets and pillows in front of the fire place which he had burning. Shyann had to admit it did look nice and no one had ever done that for her before.

" I see you went out the way."

" Naw, I didn't I just want this hour to be very special."

" I see, wheres the bathroom so I can change?" Shyann said blowing out a few of the candles Mike had lit.

" Right down the hall on the left."

" Ok, I'll be ready in 5 minutes." Shyann went into the Bathroom and undressed herself, leaving on her bra and thong. She fixed her hair and played with her make-up. She wanted this hour to fly by quickly as possible so she could get home to her girls. She put on a pair of heels, put her 38 inside her purse and took all her belongs and placed them close by her in the living room. "Run me my money." Shyann stood over Mike, holding out her hand.

" Damn, chill. I'm going to pay you." Mike reached into his robe pocket and handed Shyann 1,000$ in 20's. She counted the money and placed it in her tote bag.

" Ok, let's go. You have until 6:45 baby."

Mike grabbed Shyann and began kissing her on her breasts. He sucked her nipples and rolled his tongue all over them. Mike then lay her down in front of the fire place on the blankets and began kissing her belly button. He worked his way into her inner thighs and pulled her thong off. Shyann was getting turned on, something that she never does. She keeps business, business, but Mike was making her want it more and more.

Mike gently began kissing Shyann's pussy and she began to get wet. He stuck his tongue inside her and began rotating it inside while still inside, and ate her out. Shyann began to feel weak and wanted Mike badly, but she held her feelings and let him continue doing what he was doing. Mike continued to eat Shyann out until she cumed. Mike looked at Shyann and smiled. He reached for the condom on the table to put it on. Mike told her to turn over, Shyann did. He inserted his penis inside her vagina very slow and laid with his chest on her back. Mike took his time and made love to Shyann.

Shyann had never met a man that took time to make her feel good and Mike did just that. Mike turned Shyann over and pressed his chest against hers and continued to go nice and slow. Shyann wanted to moan and scream but her pride wouldn't allow her to do so. She felt good and didn't want the moment to end. She felt him about to cum and grabbed him closer to her. Mike cumed and lifted off Shyann to lay next to her and doubled over.

" Man. That shit is bomb." Mike said.

" Yeah, you're not to bad yourself. You still got 10 minutes left babe." Shyann said with a smile on her face.

" I know you don't cuddle, but can you just lay here? I wont touch you."

" Sure." Shyann laid there and thought about Mike and what they had just experienced. She was shocked that he made her feel the way he did.

Shyann hasn't dated anyone since Nate went away. She focused on her girls and was busy trying to provide and make sure all their needs were met as well as their wants. She felt something about this guy and didn't know what it was. Shyann was so busy thinking she didn't hear Mike talking to her.

" Hello, are you there? Can you take a shower with me?" Mike asked again.

" Oh, naw. I gotta shake. My kids waiting for me. Time up anyways." Shyann wanted to stay but had to snap into reality and tell herself this is business. "Hit me when you want to do this again, and next time I'll show you a few tricks of my own." Shyann hoped up and put on her jeans and wife beater and headed for the door.

" Wait!" Mike screamed, walking towards the door. "How was I?"

" Usually a man that questions, how they were, was whack. But in your case, your pretty good." Shyann said with a smirk on her face.

" Can we go out to dinner soon?" Mike said opening the front door for her.

" No, I don't date my customers."

" I'll pay you 500$."

Shyann is all about her paper so he knew just how to get her to say yes. "Okay, in that case, sure! I'll call you. Later." Shyann hoped in her Rover and smashed out. She got home and took a shower then went to talk to Mercedes.

" Can I come in?" She said standing at Mercedes door.

Mercedes got up to open the door for her and smiled. " Yes mama, and If I were to say no, you'll come in anyways."

" That is true huh!" They both shared a smile.

" What's up?"

" First I want to thank you for taking care of your sister and helping me around the house. You looked a little down earlier, is something wrong?"

" No, I'm okay."

" If I met you yesterday, I would believe you. But since I didn't I know your not telling me the truth. Now, what's wrong?" Shyann and the girls are very close and they talk about everything. So she couldn't understand why Cedes was holding back.

" Ok, please don't get mad. I kind of have this boy friend named Chris and he wants to have sex and I'm not ready."

" I'm not mad at all, I'm very proud of you. I bet he fed you the whole, I love you line too huh?"

" Yes."

" I just want the best for you girls, I had you at a young age and I completely understand how you feel baby. Do you want too?"

" No, I mean, maybe. Just a little but I feel like it's not the right time."

" Then go off how you feel, I can't watch you 24/7. I trust you and I know you'll do the right thing. I love you."

" I love you too mama, thanks."

" Take it slow, you have a whole life ahead of you." Shyann kisses her on the forehead and gives her a hug. "Where's Lexie?"

" In her room."

" Okay. Did you do your homework?"

" Yes, it's all done."

Shyann went to check on Lexus and see what she was doing. "Hey baby, you always watching Sponge Bob, Lexie."

" Hey mama." Lexus jumped up to give her a hug. "It don't be nothing else on, and he's funny mama."

" Where's that homework so I can check it?"

" On the desk waiting for you." Lexus said with a smile on her face. "I did it all."

" Ok, let me just look over it and make sure it's correct."

" You have to work tonight?"

" Lexus what's tonight?"

" Thursday."

" Okay, and what's mommie's schedule?"

" Wednesday, Thursday, Friday and Saturday."

" So why are you asking me if I have to work?" Shyann began tickling Lexus and she began laughing.

" Okay, okay! I forgot."

" Speaking of work, let me go get ready. I love you."

" Love you more mama. Have a good night."

    The girls doesn't know their mom is a stripper, they think she's a bartender at a bar in Hollywood. Shyann wants to keep it like that as well. She's been at Tasty, which is in Hollywood for about 5 years now. Shyann was saving up to open a bar of her own really soon and a clothing store. Shyann has really gotten addicted to the money. She racks in an average of 10,000$ a week, and stacks as much as possible. On her off days she doesn't do anything but spend time with the girls and catch up on their lives.

CHAPTER FOUR

Messing with the wrong bitch!

" Star, you're late." Ben said as she walked in.

" Ben don't you get tired of saying that, because I'm tired of hearing it. I pay my house fees so get off my back." Star said as she walked pass him to go to the locker room. Thursday nights were slow but Star always went home with more than a g. Star got dressed and went straight to the bar as usual.

" What up Lace?"

" Hey ma, you want a shot?"

" You know it girl."

" Who got the ticket on this?"

Shyann turned to a guy sitting at the bar. "Hey baby, can I get a drink?"

" Sure, just tell Lace I got you." The guy said admiring Star's body. She wore a red bikini top and a red thong.

" Thanks babe. Let me know when you ready for some dances." She took her shot and turned to talk to Lace. "Aye ma, what you know about that nigga that was at the bar last night?"

" Who?"

" The fool who got me them shots, and was throwing 100$ bills everywhere."

" Oh, Micheal." Lace said. "What you want to know. That nigga mad stacked up. He just got divorced like a year ago, his dumb ass wife was cheating on him. He divorced that bitch and left that bitch flat broke. I think they had a child or two, I ain't sure though. Why you asking about him?"

" I'm just asking, he look like he breaded up."

" Girl, hell yeah he is. I think that nigga a judge or lawyer, one of the two. His dad owned like three different businesses and when he passed away Mike inherited all that shit. He cool peoples, funny as hell when he drunk. He'll tell you his whole life story if you asked." Lace said walking away to tend to a customer on the other side of the bar.

Star had been dancing and drinking so she went into the locker room to change and freshen up. She walked in and over heard her name. When the other girls saw her silence covered the room.

" Keep talking hoes." Star said, it didn't take much to blow her high and she sober up quick. "Keep talking dusty ass bitches." Silence continued to cover the room. Star began to undress and got her baby wipes and cleaned her body. The girls that was in the locker room rolled their eyes and walked back into the club. Stacy was in the bathroom the whole time listening to the conversation. She poked her head out before she walked out.

" What's up ma?" Star said, as Stacy walked out the bathroom.

" Hey, baby. They was mad talking about you ma."

" Who?"

" Tish and her little crew. Tish was mad poppin off at the mouth though, as usual."

" That's what I'm talking about them bitches always talking shit. When I walked in I knew they was talking about me. I'm like keep talking bitches, and no body said shit. I would murder them coke sniffing hoes."

" I know, I got your back though. You always look out for me." Stacy said.

" I know ma. Check this out let's both put on all white and go this this money, fuck these hoes."

" Ok."

Star had, had enough of them hoes. She wanted to blast their asses right there but thought about her kids. Stacy got dressed and so did Star. Star told the DJ they were going to double up on stage and did just that. Star is far from a lesbo, but knew how to play the role good as hell and have you fooled. Maybe deep down inside she wanted to experience that side but never found a chick she thought was that bomb to experience it with.

Star danced on Stacy and the whole crowd gathered around the stage throwing tips. She put her head in between Stacy legs and pretended like she was eating her out. That's really when money began to fly. They danced on the pole and removed their tops. Tasty was just a topless bar so they weren't allowed to be nude. Stacy kissed Star's nipple, Star almost came out of character but remember she needed to get her paper. Star gave Stacy body language to continue and that it was okay. Stacy sucked her nipples. The crowd screamed and went crazy. Star actually enjoyed the feeling.

Ben notices a lot of noise and comes out from the back office and tells the DJ to cut the track and snatches the mic.

" Okay, shows over." Stacy and Star was so caught up in the moment they didn't hear Ben, besides the guys were really loud. Star opened her eyes and saw Ben and smile. She told Stacy to look. Stacy turned and looked at Ben and laughed. They both put each others tops on and gathered their money off the stage and went into the holding room.

" Oh my gosh." Stacy said jumping up and down laughing. "I hope we don't get fired."

" Girl, please. I'm Star. If it wasn't for me, these niggas wouldn't even be in here and this place would get no business." Star stopped and looked at Stacy in a way she never looked at a woman before. Stacy was very pretty. She was light skin, she had ass, but her chest was small, maybe 32B. She was beautiful, but very shy so they guys wouldn't talk to her very much. Star thought she could really make some money with her. Star smiled as Stacy counted the money.

" Damn, girl we made 526$."

" That's good ma, we have to do this more often. Well as long as Ben fat ass sleep somewhere." They both shared a laugh. " You real cool ma, I'm digging you. We can make some mad bread."

" That's what I'm talking about. Thanks Star." Stacy gave her a hug, and Star couldn't hold back, she squeezed her butt. Stacy didn't think nothing of it. " Okay, so you going to handle Ben?"

" Yup! Let's go"

" In my office now. The both of you." Ben snapped. As we walked pass Tish and her crew, they all had smiles on their faces.

" What the hell yall broke bitches laughing at?" Star stopped in front of them. Ben grabbed her to keep walking. "I'm tired of them hoes."

" Have a seat."

" What up Ben?"

" You know damn well we don't allow that shit. Don't let it happen again, now get out my face."

" Alright Ben dang, just trying to get a little extra cash. But we got you, wont happen again." They both walked out.

" Wow, that's it?"

" Girl, Ben don't trip off me, I do what I want, when I want. He know if I wasn't working here he wouldn't have the crowd he has, so I don't pay him no mind. I need a double." Star went to the bar and Stacy went into the locker room to change. "Double ma." She said to Lace.

" I gotcha. This one on me." Lace said smiling. "Yall killed it on stage. Tish'em was hating the whole time, I was cracking up."

" Them bent out of shape ass hoes. I got something for their asses, watch." Lace handed her the double and Star took it all in one gulp. Star made her rounds and did lap dances and mingled with the crowd. Racked out with an easy 1,300$ after pay out. Stacy asked for a ride, Star told her she had something to do but she'd drop her off right after that. Stacy agreed and smashed in the Rover with Star.

Star waited in the parking lot until Tish came out and got into her car then slowly pulled out behind her. Star followed her to her house keeping a distance and not making herself noticeable. Stacy caught on to what Star was doing and began worrying.

" Are you following her?"

" Maybe, you ain't in this car and you don't see shit, right?" Star turned to Stacy and said in a tone in which she never spoken to Stacy in.

" Your business ma."

Shyann grabbed a spray bottle she kept under the passenger seat and a box of matches from the glove department. Stacy looked like she wanted to ask her what was she going to do, but kept her mouth shut. Tish parked her car on the street and Shyann turned off her lights and stopped about four cars behind her. It was about 2:20am, Shyann grabbed the spray bottle and ran across the street. It took Tish about 3 minutes to get her things out of the car and walk across the street so that gave Shyann enough time to cross the street and duck behind the car parked in front of Tish's apartment.

Shyann heard Tish approaching and put her large hood from her hoody over her face. She didn't speak, because Tish would recognize her voice. Shyann squired the spray bottle three times in Tish's face and stroke a match and threw it on her face. Tish's whole head caught fire. The spray bottle was filled with gasoline, something Nate taught her. Shyann walked quickly to the car. She heard Tish screaming really loud and feel to the grass and began rolling around trying to stop the fire. Shyann quickly hopped in the truck and reversed down the street and made a quick right at the first corner she saw.

They both began laughing. " I can't believe you did that." Stacy said.

" Fuck that bitch, and you ain't seen shit?"

" Girl, I'm not going to say shit. Man you hood as fuck for that one."

Shyann drove to Stacy's house and they rode the rest of the ride in silence.

" Alright ma, this is your stop." Stacy's like 22, Shyann got a good 9 years on her so Stacy's anxious to hang out with her.

" I'm going to hit you up tomorrow. Thanks and good night."

" Alright. Later ma." Shyann said driving off.

Before Shyann went home she got rid of her hoddy and the spray bottle. She drove to Burbank and put it in the suwer on a dead end street. Shyann was tired and just wanted to relax and get some rest. She got in the house and ran a bubble bath and poured a glass of wine and relaxed. She didn't get in bed until about 4am and set the alarm to 6:15 to make breakfast for the girls.

When she awake the next morning, Tish's story was on the news. They said she has 3rd degree burns to the head and police has no witnesses or suspects. Tish can barely talk, her whole face was completely burned. Shyann just smiled and continued to get the girls ready for School. She continued her normal day as usual, at work no one suspected anything. She did her and got her paper.

CHAPTER FIVE

Family.

Every Sunday morning Shyann and the girls go to church. After Church Shyann's mother Megan cooks Sunday dinner so the girls spend the day there. Shyann's dad died about three years ago from cancer. Shyann's brother, Henry comes over as well. He's 26, doesn't have any kids and rips and runs the streets. Those are Megan's only two babies and only two grand kids, she'll do anything for them.

" Hey mama, you need help in here?"
" Hi, baby. I'm okay, you know I got it." Megan said smiling. "Where my girls at?"
" In there with their big head uncle."
" Oh, Henry here already."
" Yes'mam. He pulled up when we I did, I was surprised too. That boy ain't never on time."
" Who you telling, he was born 3 weeks late so I already knew what to expect." They both started laughing. Henry and the girls walk in. Lexus and Mercedes both gave their grandmother a hug and ran back into the living room.
" Hey mama, how you feeling?" Henry said, giving her a kiss.
" I'm feeling fine."
" You been taking your pills?"
" Pills for what mama?" Shyann said.
" You would know if you came around more often, little big sister." Henry said, with a fake smile on his face. "She has high blood pressure."
" Mama, why didn't you tell me." Shyann said.
" Child, no need for you worrying. You just take care of the beautiful girls. They got so big." Megan said walking out the kitchen to set the dinning room table.

" She going to be alright Henry?"
" She'll be straight, she just forget to take them sometime. How you been doing?"
" You know me, I handle mines."

" Yeah, that's true. I got some addresses on Nut and Blaze about them kilos and that 2 mill coming up missing."

" Word. Them niggas are going to pay. They probably though I forgot and shit."

" You talked to Nate lately?"

" Fuck that nigga, I went up there to see him last week and he had some bitch up there and shit. I'm cool on him, I mean I'm out here and I'm doing me and all but I ain't got no nigga. He know the day I comes up there, at least have that bitch come on a different day. What if I had the girls with me too. They would've tried to murder that hoe, well at least Mercedes. You know she crazy about her daddy."

" Aw, he doing it like that. I feel you though, have a little respect. But when you ready to run up on them niggas let me know."

" Alright."

Megan finished dinner and they all sat down to eat. Megan cooked fried pork chops, mac and cheese, greens, corn bread and yams. They enjoyed the food, laughter and each others company. Shyann phone rings and it's Stacy. She didn't answer it. She called again and Shyann got up from the table and walked into the kitchen to answer it.

" What's up?" Shyann answered with a attitude.

Stacy was crying. "This nigga just hit me."

Shyann wasn't trying to get caught up in her shit. "Your dude? Call the police ma."

" He'll kill me if I did that."

" I know you ain't scared Stacy."

" I'm just in shock and I just need to clear my head."

" Okay, you got some cash? Call a taxi and come to my moms house."

" Are you sure it's cool Star?"

" Yeah, it's straight. Don't say shit about the club though, my kids here they don't know my get down."

" Ok, I wont I promise. What's the address?"

" We on the corner of Vine and Maple 3985. You'll see my Rover parked in front. Be safe ma, and make sure that nigga don't follow you."

" Ok, I wont, thanks." They both hung up.

" Who was that Shy?" Megan asked.
" My friend Stacy. She's going to come by, she got into a fight with her dude. It's cool mama?"
" Of course child, sit down and finish eating." Megan said stuffing her mouth with greens. Shyann thought to herself, I ain't got time for this young bitch and her drama around my kids. But Shyann knows how it feels to need help and not have anyone their for them. Shyann analyzed her life and realized she was tired of working at the club and running game on niggas. Shyann had plenty of money so she could quit anytime, but she had a bad addiction. She was addicted to fast money and was in love with it.

Shyann has been through a lot with niggas trying to play her and cheating and shit. When Nate got locked up she didn't date or fuck anyone for a year. She began to get very lonely and began dating and fucking niggas. She never let it get serious though, then she got tired of niggas falling in love. She flipped the whole show, if a nigga wanted to fuck he had to pay.

Her whole attitude changed and she began to be all about her paper. Shyann got mad paper. She racks a minimum of 10 grand a week, working four days, four weeks in the month, for 5 years plus making money on the side! Niggas would buy her expensive gifts and shit, she'd return them and stack the paper. That bitch didn't have to work another day in her life if she didn't want to. What she loved most was the power over dumb ass niggas. Her Rover paid off, walked on the lot and dropped cash. Her house?. . .That bitch did that the same way, dropped 250,000 down cash.

Throughout her whole house is wooden floors and expensive furniture and custom made pieces. She has mirrors on the ceiling in her bedroom. Full walk in closet the size of a bedroom. She remodeled her whole restroom and added a full size Jacuzzi. She's doing well, she's not the flashy type, she didn't need 3 or 4 cars so people can know she got it. She cool and mellow and the bitch was balling!

CHAPTER SIX

Playing with fire.

    Wednesday night after work she drops off Stacy. She hadn't seen or heard from her since Sunday when she was suppose to come by Megan's house. Stacy said her dude apologized and they made up. Shyann wanted to tell her not to put up with that nigga, but felt she was they type of chick that needed to learn from experience. She noticed a Silver Charger was following her. She thought to herself, this mother fucker must think I'm dumb and shit. She reached in the back seat and put her 38 in her lap. Stacy saw her and her eyes grew big.

    " What's up ma?" Stacy asked.

    " This Silver Charger been on us since we left the club. I thought it was just driving in the same direction, but every turn I make it's making." Stacy positioned her body to turn around and Shyann grabbed her arm. "Don't turn around and look fool. I'm finna pop whoever it is." Shyann was very smart and a thought crossed her mind. She knew her kids ride in the truck and didn't want whoever it was to retaliate. She thought quick and called her homeboy JJ who owed her a favorite.

    " JJ, what that shit do, it's Shy."

    " What up? I'm chillin on the block, you know a nigga don't sleep. You need some?"

    " Naw, I'm good I actually stopped smoking like 3 months ago. Look, I need you to do me a favorite."

    " You know, I got you. What's up? JJ said, he stayed ready for trouble plus he like Shyann and would do anything to stay on her good side.

    " I'm about to hit the block in about 5 minutes. Some nigga following me, smoke they ass for me. It's a silver charger on 22's. You know I'm good for it but I be having my kids and shit in here and I'm not trying to put them in danger, ya feel?"

    " I got you, I'm about to get my little homies on that shit right now."

    " Good lookin', I'll take care of ya in the morning."

    " Fa'sho, Later!"

    Shyann know she's done a lot of dirt and being Nate's baby mama, he did even more. So she always assume their after her for what she did, or after her because Nate's in jail and why not get who's closer to him; which is his family. Nate taught Shyann everything she needed to know to protect herself. He knew he was heavy in the coke game and could go to jail for any little small thing. Shyann was his heart and he made her tuff, and taught her that everyone is an enemy so treat them like one. Stacy just sat in the truck, quiet. She wanted to tell Shyann to drop her off, but was afraid that she would snap at her.

    Shyann made a right on LaBrea and slowed down to 25 miles. The streets were dark and completely empty. She knew JJ and his crew was out there but couldn't see where. She looked in her rear view mirror and saw the Charger turn behind her, trying to keep it's distance and not be obvious. But little did they know Shyann was already up on it. Shyann stopped at the stop sign then continued to drive. When the Charger stopped at the stop sign, someone dressed in all black ran across the street in front of the car. Another guy also in all black ran from the back of the car to the driver's side and fired his 9 about 6 times, 2 were to the head. It was a bitch driving.
    One of the guys pushed the bitch over into the passenger seat and the other one hopped in the back seat. They drove the car to the park up the hill and took off all their clothes and poured gasoline on everything, including the car. They both stood in their boxers and set that shit on fire and ran back down the block. They told JJ what they did and said no one saw them, then went in the spot a took showers. JJ called Shy.
    " Shy, it was a bitch the little homies said. They blasted that hoe and set that bitch and her car completely on fire."
    Shyann smiled when she heard what JJ said, but was thinking who?..what bitch? "JJ, what she look like?"
    " Ma I don't even know. I'll ask the homies."
    " Alright, I'll come by in the morning and have something for ya. Good lookin' again. Later."
    " Fa'sho. Later."
    Shyann took a shower and couldn't think of who it could've been. She didn't sweat it either and didn't miss any sleep.

" What up JJ? What up Silent?" Shyann greeted them outside the apartments.

" Hey, Shy. I haven't seen you in a few months. You still look good." Silent said as he licked his lips and walked to the back of the building. Shyann just smiled.

" Here ya go." Shyann handed JJ a white envelope filled with 20$ bills totaling 10,000$.

" Awww, Shy you didn't have too."

" I know but I did, so take it and shut up." She said with a grin. "Thanks again my nigga. Did yo' boys say what she looked like?"

" They said that shit happened so fast, but the bitch was light skin and had blonde hair."

" Damn, I can't think of nobody." She put her hand on her head trying to think.

" Yeah, but that bitch gone now, so fuck her." JJ laughed. "That's what the hoe get for fucking with you. Niggas better know your ass is crazy and don't play."

" I am not, I just don't tolerate nascence and dumb ass people that want to fuck with me."

" I feel you, Shy." He said admiring her little outfit.

She wore a pair of shorts and a button down shirt that exposed her breasts, with a pair of Steve Madden boots with a 3" heel. She looked casual but cute, and if you let JJ tell it she was sexy. JJ wasn't bad looking his self. He had 2 dimples that brought his smile out, he was also light skin and always keep fresh corn rolls. He was much younger than Shyann though, by 7 years. He didn't care, he really liked her. JJ was Nate's little homie and had a crush on Shy since the first day he saw her. With JJ being in jail, he thought about trying to hook up with her, but he respected Nate too much to dog him like that.

" I'm out." JJ grabbed her by the hand and put a dub bag of purple cush in her hand and smiled.

" Relieve some stress Shy, I'm sure that's what Nate would say if he were here. You're handling your business and I just thought it was about time someone told you. Be safe Shy, and hit me if you need me." Shyann smiled because JJ was telling the truth. Shyann never shows weakness and pushes hard for her and her kids.

" Thanks." Shyann kissed JJ on the cheek and looked him in his eyes. She couldn't resist his juicy pink lips, and kissed him. JJ was excited inside and grabbed the back of her neck and began kissing her back. Shyann tried to pull back and JJ wouldn't let her.

" JJ! JJ!" She moaned with JJ's tongue in her mouth. He opened his eyes and removed his mouth from hers.

" Shit! My fault Shy." Shyann gently shoved him and they laughed.

" Nigga. Bye!"

" What?" He yelled as she walked away. "It ain't my fault you so damn hot and sexy."

CHAPTER SEVEN

Keep yo' mouth shut!

Few days passed and word around the club was some niggas wife that be coming up here was set on fire. Stacy told Star she was nervous and wanted to know if she said anything.

" Bitch, shut the fuck up. I ain't said shit and don't know what the fuck they talking about, and you don't either."

" I know, I'm just saying. Everyone talking about it up here and shit."

" Bitch you didn't do shit and neither did I, so what the fuck yo' young ass scared of." Star had been getting tired of this young hoe and wished she'd shut the fuck up and chill before she had to take that bitch out. Star didn't befriend many bitches, cause all hoes do is talk, talk and talk.

When she first saw Stacy, she looked out for her when the other girls tried to walk over her and shit. Star ain't never asked that bitch for shit. So she at least thought the bitch would keep her mouth shut. To this day all of Star friends were males, only females she felt she had to deal with was her mother, and her daughters. Besides that she'll murder a bitch quick as fuck for coming to close and trying to get in cool with her.

She though, maybe it was a nigga that she fucked or is still fucking wife that was looking for her. That bitch would've been better off just living with the fact that he was fucking someone else. She laughed inside, and a smile appeared on her face.

" Why you smiling ma?" Lace said from behind the bar.

" Because these bitches wasting valuable time talking about a dead niggas bitch and I'm about to snatch up all this money in here. Give me a double Lace."

" I heard that, who got this ticket ma?"

Star put her hand on this white guy's shoulder sitting at the bar, next to where she was standing. "You got this one babe." She told the guy and grabbed the double and began making her paper.

She hit the stage looking fierce and money began to rain all over her falling landing on the stage. When she danced on stage she felt high and mighty, like everyone praised her and she was the center of attention. She knew just how to move her body to make niggas eyes become stuck. The other girls in the club just sat around and hated on her, for indeed she was the best and they knew it.

She gathered her money off the stage and headed off, the girls envied her walk, her attitude and her swag. They wanted to be her and make the money she was making, but Star had that whole club locked down.

Shyann drove to Pasadena to meet one of her customers. Foster would call Shyann once every other month or so. He worked a lot and didn't have time to date, so he kept Shyann a phone call away. She agreed to meet him at his house as usual, Shyann didn't feel like going but when money called she got up and got it.

Foster lived well, he was divorced with three kids. He found out his wife was cheating on him and kicked her out along with the kids. He don't give a shit about no one but himself. He's waiting on the DNA testes to find out if the kids are really his. An average day for Foster is simple, work, drink, eat, then sleep and do the same thing again the next day. He works 6 days a week, doing between 14-16hours.

Shyann walked up to the building and went to apartment number 7 and rang the doorbell. Foster came to the door smelling like beer, and his speech was very sluggish.

" Hey girl!" Foster said smiling.

" What's up, you look wasted." Shyann said as she walked in.

" You want something to drink."

" Nope. I'm finna change and I'll be ready in 5. You got my money?"

" Dang girl, you don't change huh?" He said smiling.

" Nope." Shyann went into the bathroom and undressed herself and put on her heels. Foster went into the kitchen and took 400$ out of a cookie jar.
When Shyann came out the restroom he was sitting on the couch with the money in his hand.

" Here!" Shyann walked over and counted the money.
" Fasho, you ready?" Shyann asked.
" Yeah, come here." Foster began rubbing on his dick and licking his lips. He began to get hard and Shyann began stroking his dick with her hand.
" You like that?"
" Yeahh!" Foster moaned, he reached for a condom and put it on. "Sit on it."
They began having sex, all that went through Shyann's head was the time. She paid attention to every minute that passed for she knew, it was going to be over soon. Foster began to get rough with Shyann and began to pump very hard.
" Aye nigga, not so rough." Shyann snapped. "I don't know what the fuck you think this is." Foster grabbed Shyann and began sucking on her neck. "Nigga, what did I just say? You know I don't go for all that shit, we ain't making love." Foster didn't pay her any mind he continued to be rough. Shyann slapped him across the face and got up off his dick.
" What the fuck, I still got 10 minutes." Foster shouted.
" Nigga, who the fuck you getting loud with. You know the rules, now you can wait time talking or you can finish. Don't fucking put your hands on me again or I'll fucking kill you."
Foster began laughing. "Come on, I'm sorry. Dang!" Shyann lay back down on the couch and Foster got on top. He stroked his dick to get back hard.
" You got like 5 more minutes and I'm out." Foster slid in and began pumping and pumping until he came. When he finished Shyann pushed him off her and stood up.
" Don't ever pull no shit like that again, this my show and my call nigga!" Shyann snapped.

" Bitch please!"

" What did you call me?"

" The sex good and all but you got a fucked up ass attitude and you need to keep that shit to yourself."

" Nigga, you got me fucked up. I'll show you a bitch." Shyann walked in the bathroom.

" Hurry up so you can bounce, I'm done fucking with you bitch. Imma get me another prostitute, because that's all you are." He had pushed Shyann's patience with that comment. She quietly opened the bathroom door to see where he was at.

Foster was standing in front of the refrigerator bent over reaching for a Miller from the back. Shyann took her pocketknife from her purse and stood behind him. He stood up to close the refrigerator door and Shyann sliced his neck from behind. Foster dropped the beer and it fell to the floor.

" Bitch, you fucking bitch." He mumbled. The sound of bitch coming out his mouth into her ears disgusted her and turned her stomach. Shyann sliced him in the throat again. Blood gushed out and flew all over the kitchen. Shyann stabbed him in his right leg, then his left.

Foster held his throat with both hands and stood with his mouth open. Shyann kicked him and he fell to the ground. She stood over him and watched the flood flow from his neck and his legs. She began to laugh out loud.

" Nigga, hurry up and die so I can go please." Foster began to spit up blood and a few minutes later she stopped moving. Shyann took a butcher knife from her drawer and chopped his head off on the forth try. She swung the knife behind her head and with all her might and power went through and his head disconnected from his body.

She had blood all over her, she cleaned up her mess and made sure not to leave any finger prints behind. She searched his house and found 12,000$ in under his bed in a safe. Shyann wasn't a thief, but that nigga played her so she did what she felt was necessary in this situation. 12,000$ was chump change to her, she didn't need it at all. Shyann didn't care about nobody but herself, and was a cruel murderer.

CHAPTER EIGHT

All Smiles.

May approached fast and it was Mercedes birthday. Shyann wanted to get her something very special. She had been doing excellent in School and had gotten all A's and one B. Shyann parked a white Monte Carlo fully stocked on 20's in front of the School, with a huge red bow on it. The back window read, "Cedes' Baby" in light pink cursive writing. The rims were all white with light pink outlining. The leather seats were off white with light pink trimmings. The bell rang and all the students began to walk out of the main entrance. She stood waiting for Mercedes, about 3 minutes later Mercedes walked out the School holding Chris hand. She saw her mama and ran to her with a look of surprise.

" Oh, my goodness. Mama!" She yelled jumping up and down. All the students surrounded her and Shyann. "Mama, mama." She smiled. "Is this for me?"

Shyann smiled and gave her a hug. "Happy Birthday baby."

" Can I drive?" Shyann handed her the keys and Mercedes ran to the drivers seat. She totally forgot that she was walking with Chris and drove off. Shyann began teaching Mercedes how to drive when she the turned 15. So she knew she could handle the Monte Carlo.

" Thank you so much mama. I'm so happy, now I'm really the hottest chick on the squad." She laughed.

" Girl, shut up." Shyann smiled. "Okay, so you know it's rules."

Mercedes rolled her eyes. "Of, course."

" School and back and on the weekend you have to ask can you drive. I got this book from the dmv." She handed her the Written Test study guide. "Study and I'll take you in a few days to get your permit."

" Ok, thanks mom." They drove a few blocks to Lexus School to pick her up. Lexus was standing out front of the School and stared at the unfamiliar car as Mercedes stopped. When Shyann put her head out the window. Lexus smiled, her eyes grew big when she saw the bow.

" Wow." Lexus yelled. Shyann got out the car to lift the seat up and let Lexus in. "Happy Birthday Cedes." She said giving her a kiss on the cheek. "I love your new car, when I get 16 I'm going to get one too mama said."

" Mama can I go out later please, I'll be extra careful." Mercedes asked. Shyann wanted to tell her no, but figured just this once.

" Ok, but. ."

" Thanks mama."

" I said, but, you are not about to be out all night and you can't be driving all over town. You do not have your drivers license and if you wreck this car I will kick yo' ass, you'll never drive again. Got it?"

" Yes, can I have some money." Mercedes smiled. Shyann reached in her purse and handed her 100 dollars.

" Be careful."

Your call!

" Are you sure your ready to take this test?" Shyann asked Mercedes as they stood in line.

" Yes. I been studying and plus my friend took hers and she said it was super easy." She said flipping the pages in the study guide. She handed the book to her mama and went to take the test. Shyann said a prayer within that she'll pass. About 20 minutes later Mercedes returned to where Shyann was standing in the waiting area. She walked up with a big koo-laid smile.

" I passed." Mercedes said smiling and overly excited.

" Good. I'm happy for you. I need to stop at the store, feel like driving?"

" Yup!" She answered quickly.

They pulled up to the grocery store and went in. Mercedes pushed the basket and Shyann placed the items in the cart. She saw someone she knew, she really didn't care for the bitch so she didn't speak. They lady noticed her and gave her a fake smile and approached her.

" Hey, Shy." Ashley said.

" What's up." Shyann said placing a gallon of milk into the basket.

" I been calling you." Shyann found out some fowl shit about Ashley and stop talking to that bitch. Ashley never was her home girls but Ashley would always pretend like they were close and shit. Ashley used to be around the hood because she was fucking on Nate's homie. So they would see each other from time to time. Shyann dropped her off one day and Ashley asked to exchange numbers. Shyann didn't think shit of it so, she did. When Nate got arrested for that murder rumors on the block and shit was that she snitched. When Shyann ran up on her in her crib she denied it. Surprisingly for some unknown reason she convinced Shy she didn't snitch because if she did they would've used her as a witness, and some other bull shit. Since that day Shy told herself she just wasn't going to fuck with her.

Dusty hoe!

    For the last month Ashley been calling her, and she hasn't been answering. Shyann thought, if it's important the bitch would leave a message. Once you fucked over Shy or gave her reason to doubt trusting you, you fucked up with her forever. She was sincere enough to forgive people of their wrong doings, but never will forget.

    " I've been busy." Shyann put her hand on her hip. "What's up, what you need?"

    " Shit, you been on my mind heavy lately. I wanted to know what you been up to?" Shyann felt this bitch was up to something. She didn't trust anyone.

    " Cedes go get some cheese for me." Mercedes rolled the basket to get the cheese on the opposite end of the aisle. "See ya' round." Shyann turned to walk away and Ashley grabbed her arm.

    " I know you ain't still mad about what happened about Nate. Let's chill and smoke a blunt like we used too." Shyann reached in her purse and grabbed the bag JJ gave her when a few weeks ago.

    " Naw, I'm cool. I'm hanging with my girls tonight. But here ma' I got some cush, I quit a few months ago." Shyann put the bag in Ashley's hand and walked to meet Mercedes by the cheese.

    " Alright girl." Ashley turned and walked away.

    Shyann is smart and always got tricks up her sleeve. Later that night after JJ gave her that bag. Shyann went home and sprayed roach spray on the cush. She was going to give it to any grimy bitch that fucked with her at the club. Them hoes be so high and drunk they'd accept free cush any day. It's been a few weeks so the smell shouldn't be that strong she thought. That's and old trick she picked up from Nate years ago. The nigga that smoked that shit went 51/50 and was mentally damaged for life. Shyann smiled to herself and thought, one day hopefully people will learn.

    They swung by to pick up Lexus from School and went home. Shyann surprised both they girls with iPhones. Since Mercedes was now driving she needed to make sure they could communicate, and she got one for Lexus so she wont feel left out. Shyann cooked dinner and ate with the girls, then left for work.

CHAPTER NINE

Grown huh?! 11:00pm

" What if I came through the window? I really miss you." Chris said over the phone.

" Well, maybe. How are you going to get here?"

" My mama car. If we didn't have a car, girl I'll run over there for you. It's just like 20 blocks." They both giggled together. " Ok. I'll be there in 30minutes."

" Ok, come to the side of the house, my window will be open. Come in quietly and quickly so no one will see you. I love you."

" I love you too, Cedes." Chris hung up. Mercedes ran to the bathroom to take a shower. She put on a royal blue bra and royal blue under wears to match, that read "kiss me" in front of her vagina. She lay in the bed and waited for Chris to come in. About 5minutes later Chris came through the window.

" Hey."

" Hey, sit down right here." Mercedes tapped on the bed.

" I miss you."

" Me too, so you ready?" Mercedes asked nervously.

" Yes." Chris looked her in the eyes and began tongue kissing her. He rubbed her breasts and went down to her vagina. He began kissing her on the neck and removing his clothing.

" Wait! Lock the door Chris." Chris didn't want to break the moment, but had no choice. He stood in front of the door and removed his boxers and placed his hand on his dick and began to rub himself. He walked back to the bed and removed her under wear and began kissing her on her neck. He moved down to her belly button and kissed her pussy lips. Mercedes was so wet by now. She enjoyed the feeling and didn't want Chris to stop.

She put her hand on Chris head as he began eating her out. She began to melt, he loved the way her fresh pussy tasted. He moved his tongue down by her anal and put it in and ate her ass out. Juices poured out of her pussy fast as she exploded. She began to moan and grind her hips. Chris came up and whispered, "I love you."

Chris spread her legs to insert his penis.

" Wait! We have to use a condom, I'm not ready for kids."

" Ok, baby." Chris reached into his jean pocket and grabbed the condom and put it on. Mercedes lay there, and he inserted his penis in really show.

" Ouch!" Mercedes screamed.

" Sorry, Am I going to hard?" Chris said as he stopped.

" No, go ahead. It's ok."

He began to go in slow and after a few pumps the pain eased. Mercedes began to bleed and got nerves.

" I'm not suppose to have my period for 2 more weeks."

" I'm popping your cherry Cedes, it's ok. It's normal my mama told me." Mercedes continued moaning and pulled Chris closer. Chris was about to cum so the speed of his pumps went faster. Mercedes began to moan and holler.

" Ok! Ok!" Just as she said that Chris came and lay on top of her. She tried to lift him up and move him, but she was too weak.

" Get up. Chris!" She yelled. Chris rolled off her. "That was it?" She asked looking under the covers. She thought to herself, damn it felt better when he ate me out.

" That was good." Chris said loosing breath.

" I need to clean this mess and take a shower."

" Can I join you?" Chris asked.

" Come on." She smiled.

They tip-toed down the hallway to the bathroom and showered together. Mercedes took the bloody sheets off the bed and put them in a plastic bag and told Chris to dump them down the street somewhere. She figured her mama wouldn't notice them missing. She put a fresh clean sheet on and kissed Chris good night.

" See you tomorrow."

" Can I take this?" Chris held up her royal blue bra he took off earlier.

" I guess." She said smiling. She went to bed smiling and couldn't stop thinking about Chris and how good he made her feel. She couldn't believe she went through with it.

Mercedes and Chris had been hanging out a lot while her mom was at work. One night Lexus got up to use the bathroom in the middle of the night and heard voices from Mercedes. Lexus opened the door and saw Chris in the bedroom with her.

" I'm telling mama!" Lexus yelled.

" Lexus wait, no. Please don't." Mercedes replied.

" I'm going to leave, see you tomorrow at School." He kissed Mercedes on the forehead and left through the window.

" I'm telling! I'm telling. You know mama doesn't like for us to have boys over."

" Wait! I'll do anything you ask. Please don't tell." Mercedes cried. "She'll kill me."

" I can't think of nothing now, but when I do, I'll let you know." Lexus rolled her eyes and walked out the room. Mercedes didn't know what to do. She went into Lexus room and sat on her bed.

" You promise you want tell, Lexie?"

" I'm not going to tell. Pinky promise." Lexus turned her head and closed her eyes. "Good night."

" Nite, Lexie." Mercedes said as she turned the light off and pulled the door close.

CHAPTER TEN

Make it happen.

Summer was quickly approaching and School would be out for the girls. Lexus wanted to go to camp with her School for 3 weeks. Shyann didn't want her to go, but Lexus was really excited about the trip so she let her go. Mercedes told her mom that she got a summer job at the park. Shyann thought that was a great way for her to learn a little responsibility.

Shyann took the summer off from "Tasty" and focused on her urban clothing store she was working on. She found a space for rent on Sunset, she was really excited about that. She thought for a year she'll rent, and if the business is good she'll buy. She planned to have the grand opening in July so this gave her a few weeks to get everything together. Megan gave her a number of a close friend she knew in the same business to help her.

Shyann just pretty much gave them all her ideas and they put everything together for her. She had clothes like Roca Wear, Baby Phat, Ecko, Guess, Phat Farm, Sean John and so many more. She had handbags, accessories, heels and sneakers. Shyann was the one that wanted to do the hiring though. She couldn't find anyone she could trust. Megan gave her a few numbers of some people looking for work from her Church. Three out of the five people she thought she'd give a chance.

" I want to work at the store mama." Mercedes said as they all sat and ate dinner.

" You do? Maybe that can work out. When School starts back you can work after School." Shyann replied.

" I want to work too." Lexus wined.

" Come'on Lexus, you know you're too young." Shyann said.

Grand opening.

friends and family gathered on the sidewalk on sunset in front of "Shy's urban wear". It was 11am and everyone was anxious to go inside and see the store.

" Okay, hi everyone. Thanks for coming out to my grand opening today. I'm aiming for success and a new reason to live. I want to dedicate this store to two very special young women in my life, Lexus and Mercedes." The crowd began to cheer. "They are the reason why I push everyday and never give up." her eyes filled with tears, Shyann rarely cried and showed weakness, but she couldn't control her emotions. "i know i be hard on you girls but I love you guys and this is for yall!" She took the big scissors and cut the red ribbon from the door. "Alright, go shop."

Lexus and Mercedes both gave their mama a hug and kiss. "We love you." Mercedes said.

" Mama we should have named it, Lexie's. that would have been perfect." They began to giggle and smile. The store was very huge, one side was painted pink for the woman and girls and the other half was blue for men and boys. Mirrors flowed through all the walls and dressing rooms. As everyone ran in to shop, she stood at the door and smiled.

" Thank you Jesus." She whispered to herself and went inside her store.

School was just a few weeks away. Shyann decided to quit working at "Tasty's". Mike wasn't happy when Shyann told him that she's getting out the business. He offered her more money and she turned him down. Mike was very disappointed, he had fallen in love with her. Shyann didn't pay him any attention, her focus was on the store.

Business at the store was great and she enjoyed being a business woman. She had just closed up and was heading home when her cell rang.

" Hello", she answered.

" What's up girl, it's Stacy!"

" What's up ma? you still at the club?"

" Yeah. The money too good to leave, ya know. I was just calling because I heard you opened a store and wanted to spend some money with you."

" Oh, yeah I did a little over a month ago. It's on sunset next to the Gucci store, called Shy's. Who told you I opened a store ma, I don't talk to them hoes up there?"

" Ummm, I don't remember. I think Tish home girl Meeka or Bree. But yeah, fa'sho I'm going fuck with you. I know this trick who wants to spend some money on me."

" Oh, I didn't know you fucked with them grimy ass bitches like that. They fake."

" Girl, everybody fake." she laughed. "Besides they cool, they not as bad as Tish was. They told me that bitch whole face fucked up, she don't even go outside. They asked her who did it and she said she don't know, but when she find out she's going to kill'em."

" That bitch ain't going to do shit! She lucky whoever did it spared her life. She just need to live her pathetic life and die."

" Okay girl, I feel you. I'll come up there tomorrow. Bye!" Stacy hung up the phone.

Shyann thought Stacy was going to open her fucking mouth. Stacy was hanging tuff with Meeka and Bree and knew some shit was going to go down. Her phone rings again.

" Hello."

" What's up ma?" It was JJ.

" What's up nigga?"

" You know my birthday next week and I was inviting you to the club."

" Oh, fasho'. I'll come through. Where?"

" Vice, baby where else would I be seen?" JJ laughed. "Oh, yeah before I forget to tell you, you remember your home girl Ashley."

" That fowl bitch isn't my home girl."

" I'm just playing with you, but that bitch flipped out. I mean straight 51/50." He began to laugh. "That's what that bitch get though."

" Aww, fo'real!" Pretending to act surprised and in shock. "Damn, what happened?"

" Nobody knows she jus flipped out. But look ma, let me get back to this money. I'll holla at you soon."

" Later!" Shyann hung up.

Her phone rang again and it was Mike, she pressed ignore. She was tired of hearing that damn thing ring so she turned it off.

Chapter Eleven

Let's go back a little and find out who she was.

Shyann was on her way to her client James. James was a married man from time to time he'll hit up Shyann and have her come through. James worked as a game designer, so he was paid. This evening he called Shyann over because he was bored and his wife flew to New York for a business meeting.

" Hey, James." Shyann smiled as James answered the door.

" Man, I missed you. Good sex with no strings attached. I love it!" James said as she walked in and he closed the door.

" Let me use the bathroom and I'll be ready in about 5." Shyann went into the restroom and undressed to just her bra and thong. She put her heels on and fixed her hair. Then she walked into the den where James was.

" Sexy." James screamed as he lay on the coach. "Here." He handed Shyann an envelope with money that totaled 400$. She counted it and put it in her bag and got on top of him. She began kissing him on the neck and once he got hard they had sex.

James wife, Michelle, had reason to believe that he was cheating. He would make up excuses not to make love with her, come in really late and one night he came in smelling like woman's perfume. Michelle was a very caring person and gave her husband her all. She was beautiful; she was mixed with Indian and black. Nice shape, hazel eyes and long pretty blond hair.

The investigator was sitting outside their home when Shyann pulled up. He took photos of her and James. He wanted more photos so he took pictures through the den's window. He wrote down the time she got there and what time she left.

" That was great. I wish my wife put it on me like you do." James said. Shyann grabbed her bag and went to the bathroom to get dressed. When she was ready to leave James walked her to the door. By this time the investigator was in his car and was preparing to follow Shyann to get more photos and information about her.

" Ok, see you later." Shyann said as she walked to her truck. James watched her as she got in her truck, he noticed a white guy sitting across the street in an old black Mercedes. He didn't pay it any mind though; he thought maybe he was lost or waiting for someone.

Shyann was off from the club that night but noticed the car was following her so she drove to the club. She went in and had a few drinks and talked to lace for a little while. It was kind of crowed, so lace couldn't talk to her for very long. The investigator went inside the club about 5 minutes after Shyann and watched her from the opposite side. Shyann got a razor from her purse and headed towards the locker room to exit without being seen. She looked in the parking lot for the old black Mercedes; she spotted it and slashed all four tires. She did it really quickly and walked normally to her truck and got in. when she pulled out the driveway she saw a white tall skinny male walk towards the Mercedes. She laughed inside and drove off. She wondered who the guy was because she has never seen him before.

When Michelle got back in town the investigator showed her the photos and gave her the address to Tasty's.
" This is how she looks and I have reason to believe that she works at this place. Some of the guys were asking her if she was working tonight and could they get a dance. She drives a black range rover with black rims. Here is a picture of the vehicle. I'm sorry Mrs. Thomas but your husband is having an affair."
" I can't believe that, and with this stripper." Michelle began to cry on his shoulder. Inside she felt lost and betrayed by James. She wanted to meet Shyann herself and ask her if she knew he was married and how she could sleep with a married man.
" I have to go, I have other jobs. Once again, I am so sorry. If you still need my services call me." He hugged her and walked to his car. A couple days later Michelle became brave enough to try and face Shyann. She waited outside the club until she got off and followed her in her sliver charger!

I'm sure if she could relive that night and get her life back, she would.

Chapter Twelve

Things are looking good.

" Hey girl." Stacy said as she walked in Shyann's store.

" Hi, mama." Shyann said as Stacy gave her a hug. Stacy walked in with an older guy wearing a suit looking like a pimp or something.

" This my baby, Joseph." Shyann shook his hand. "This Shyann baby."

" Well baby go get what you want." Joseph told Stacy.

She began searching through the racks picking up everything she found in her size. Then she headed to the shoe section and got 3 pairs of shoes as well. When she was ready to check out Mercedes rang her up and her total was $1,354.83. Stacy was very greedy and didn't give a damn because it wasn't her money. Shyann thought to herself, she must be fucking for free, bitch pay for your own shit.

" Alright girl, come up to the club soon ma, I miss you."

" Bye!" Shyann said with a look of disgust on her face. Shyann told her don't say shit about the club around her kids. Even though Stacy didn't know that Mercedes was her daughter, common sense should have told her. Or maybe the bitch was so fucking drunk or high to notice a child just cashed her out.

" Mama she looks like a hooker." Mercedes said laughing.

" Shut up, you so silly." Shyann laughed with her. "I'm about to make a drop at the bank cedes then go home. Stanley on break and Melissa is in the back. I'm about to call her up here to help you. Make sure you lock up and you all leave at the same time; don't forget to set the alarm. Call me if you need me."

" Ok, mama. I love you." Mercedes said as she kissed her on the cheek.

Lexus was at Megan's house so Shyann went to the bank then went to pick her up. When she pulled up she saw Henry's car. Henry was walking out and walked up to her truck.

" Hey, shy. Man we got a location on them niggas. When you down?"

" Alright, let's hit they ass this weekend." Shyann said getting out of her truck.

" Fa'sho. I'm going to call you later."
" Ok, love ya, be safe."
" I'm always safe, love you too." Henry walked to his car and drove off.

" Mama." Lexus ran to meet her mom at the door. "Hi, mama."
" Hey, baby."
" Hey mama."
" Go get your stuff." Shyann said walking in the kitchen where Megan was.

" Hey mama. How you feeling?" Shyann said as she kissed her on the forehead.
" I'm doing well. How's the store going?"
" Good, Mercedes working tonight."
" No, don't be having that baby working all late."
" Mercedes is smart mama, she good. She likes it though, and it's good to have someone you can trust."
" You got security?"
" Mama, yes! Hollywood isn't a bad area anyways so she good. Alright mama, we about to go, love you."
" Alright if you say so shy, love you too." Megan turned to Lexus. "Excuse me miss, I know you about to kiss me bye."
" Yes, granny. Love you." Lexus kissed her on the cheek.
" Love you too."

Mercedes and the other workers were locking up the store and preparing to go home.
" Night guys, thanks."
" Goodnight." they replied.
She wanted to see Chris before she went home so she called him.
" Hey baby."
" What's up girl?" Chris replied.
" Girl? Ok!. . .what are you doing? I wanted to see you for a little while before I went home I just left the store."
" Oh, well maybe another night, I'm busy." Chris shined her off.

" Oh, ok. Later then."

" Later." Mercedes stared at the phone and wondered what his problem was.

Saturday night.

Shyann got dressed and ready to slide through JJ's party. She wasn't going to stay long because she had to meet Henry at midnight to get nut and blaze. She pulled her hair into a high ponytail. She wore an all black one-piece jean spaghetti strap backless Ecko outfit, with a pair of all black Ecko 4" heels. She kissed her kids goodnight and headed to Hollywood to club vice.
The line was long as hell; she valet parked her car and called JJ.

" Hey, happy birthday."

" Thanks baby, you coming right?"

" I'm here already, come get me this line long as hell."

" Fa'sho, I'm coming now." Shyann waited by the bouncer and told him her friend was coming out to get her.

" Aye B let her in." JJ yelled. The bouncer removed the rope and let Shyann in.

" What's up?" JJ said to Shyann as they walked in, yelling over the music.

" I need a drink, I got some shit to do later so I'm going to shake early."

" Awww, ok it's cool ma, at least you came."

" A lot of people love your ass." Shyann smiled. "It's crowed."

" Let's get you a drink and dance." Shyann knew she had to handle business so she just ordered a shot. JJ was on her all night he enjoyed her company. They danced and laughed all night. Some girl kept eyeballing her while she was with JJ, but she didn't pay her any attention for she knew her 38 was in the truck if the bitch wanted problems.

" When we going to hook up shy?" JJ screamed.

" What?" Shyann yelled, pretending she couldn't hear him. She knew he was drunk and now he was talking out the side of his ass.

" Man, I want you ma."

" This is my song." she tried to change the subject.

" I love you, you probably think I'm drunk and talking shit. I'll tell you tomorrow." he laughed and grabbed her closer to him to dance. Shyann likes JJ but wouldn't do Nate like that that was his little homie.

" I'm about to leave in a few minutes JJ, I have to meet Henry."

" Awww, tell my nigga I said what's up. Alright one more dance and you can go."

" Boy, I been dancing with you all night, I don't want your girlfriend to get mad at me."

" Girlfriend? I ain't got one of those, only person in here that might get mad is my wifey." JJ smiled.

" That bitch right there keep staring at me." she pointed her finger to the girl.

"And, let me leave before wifey gets mad." she pulled away and he grabbed her back.

" You're wifey!" he whispered and kissed her on the neck. "And, that bitch is always on my dick."

" Bye fool." she said and walked away.

She left the club at 11:40 to meet Henry on 10th ave at TK's house. She pulled up at midnight and TK and Henry was standing outside smoking a blunt.

" What's up yall?" Shyann said as she hopped out the truck.

" What up." they both replied.

" Yall ready?"

" Yeah, one second, we almost finish with this blunt." Henry said.

" So what's the plan? We just about to run up in their spot and blast them nigga?" Shyann asked.

" Naw, well kind of." TK replied.

" We about to be in and out. Snatch up all bread and dope, cush whatever up in there, smoke them niggas and shake."

" It don't be a lot of people over there?" Shyann asked Henry.

" Nope, I been watching them for the last 2 months. They stop serving at about 11, it be nut, blaze and a bitch in there after that counting paper and smoking and shit. I take nut, TK you take blaze and you take the bitch."

" Hell naw, fuck that hoe. I want nut or blaze." Shyann yelled.

" Man, would you just listen to me. Damn! You think you so damn hard." Henry snapped.

" It ain't about being hard nigga, I got heart homie and I'm blasting nut or blaze."

" Man, what did I just say Shyann! Stick to the plan or we ain't doing this shit."

TK knew not to get involved in their disagreement, plus that nigga was high and didn't want them blowing that shit on bullshit. He figured, what's the point of arguing over who gonna kill who, when all them niggas was about to die.

Shyann let Henry feel like he had the last word and that it was going to go down how he wanted it too. She was going to blast one of the niggas and didn't give a fuck what Henry was talking about.

" Ok, big little bro. It's your way." she shot him with a fake smile and folded her arms. "Let's roll, I have to get home to my girls."

They rode in a bucket TK bought like 2 weeks ago from a Mexican in the hood for like 300$.

" This shit is indeed a piece of shit TK." Shyann said as she got in.

" This piece of shit is good enough to do the job so we good. I'm going to give this shit away soon as we done with it so don't trip. Everybody ain't able to do it big like you are." TK said laughing.

" Shut up, I work hard for the shit I got and get nigga." Shyann snapped.

" I know you do ma, and you doing good. I was just fucking with you." TK looked at her through the rear view mirror.

" Alright yall, don't forget the plan, Shyann!" Henry said.

" Get off me nigga, I got you." Shyann replied.

" Make a right up here, then at the first stop sign make a left." Henry directed. Shyann had her 38 and TK and Henry both had their 9's. Shyann still had on her outfit from the club, so she debated where to put her heat, she thought fuck it, it'll just carry it at my side.

" Alright, yall see this red Tahoe, that's the building right there on the right. Park right here." Henry pointed to the building to the left of it. "We in, we out! Yall ready?"

The streets were empty just as Henry said they'd be. "I'm ready!" Shyann said.

" Let's go." TK said as they quietly got out of the car. Henry signaled 1, meaning apartment one.

TK knocked on the door.

" Yeah." a female said.

" Can I get that?" TK said through the door.

" What?"

" I need a hit, please open I don't want to make a scene." he made a point so she opened the door.

" Shyann walked in first and gave her 2shots to the head real quick and that bitch feel to the floor. Blaze was sitting on the coach with his eyes closed and the shots made him awake. He saw the girl fall to the floor and he reached for his pistol that was on the table. Shyann already had her eyes on him and gave him 2 shots to his head as well. Shots fired to the living room from the hallway and Shyann ducked and fired back. Henry began to get off as well.

" Man, in and out!" Henry yelled. "Fuck! TK kill that nigga I'll cover you." TK nodded his head and ducked and made his way to the hallway.

Henry and Shyann kept busting, TK sneaked up on Nut and shot that nigga in his chest. Shyann came up from behind and with her last bullet and shot that nigga in the head. Henry was in the living room getting the money and dope off the table.

" We out." Henry yelled and they ran to the car a drove off. They heard sirens and got out of there quickly as possible. They drove to an alley by TK's house and parked the car then walked a block to TK's house. He saw a bumb on the curb by the gas station.

" Hold on." He ran across the street and handed him the car key. "Want a car? It's one block over on Mayton Ave, you can have it, and it's in the alley."

" Thanks." The homeless guy said smiling with a mouth full of rotten teeth.

" Alright we can go now." TK said.
" You had to kill'em huh? Henry said.
" Fuck you!" Shyann snapped. "Fuck them niggas. Fuck anybody that don't have a place in my heart."
" Fuck me huh? You need to slow your roll." Henry said.
" Aye, my fault. It wasn't like that. Them niggas got what they deserved, stealing from my kids."
" Stealing from your kids or stealing from you. What you so mad fo'?. . .cause you had to get off your ass and hustle for them? Or because some nigga didn't just hand you over 2million dollars shy? Get your shit together and slow your fucking roll, stop acting like you untouchable and shit. Because reality check is, you're not!"
" What the fuck is your problem? Is little big brother jealous of little big sis?. . Hmm, I wonder. I don't want nobody to hand me shit. I love my fucking kids to death, and I'll hustle any day for their asses. The shit I go through and got to put up with is worth it all seeing my babies smile. So a nigga ain't got to hand me shit! Because reality is, I'm going to take it! Let that shit soak in nigga, and you'll need me before I'll need you." she said and walked away.
TK just pasted with Henry and she disappeared into the dark. "What's up with yall lately?"
" Man, I'm tired of her Ms. Perfect ass and her salty ass ways." Henry answered. "It's family though, so I have to deal with it. I'll talk to her later. Let's just hurry up and get back to yo' spot and count this money."
" Fa'sho."

When they got back to TK's. Shyann's truck was gone. They went upstairs and counted the money. They also took 2 sandwich bags full of dope. The money totaled 25,000.

" Damn, that's it?" Henry snapped. "I should have searched the place, I know they had more in there."

" Man if we would've did that, the one time would've caught our asses for' real. It's cool, we'll split this 3 ways, and another lick will come up." TK said. TK was cool and laid back, to him money wasn't shit. That nigga hustled so hard; paper should be his last name.

" Naw, nigga, 2 ways. Nobody told shy to leave."

" Whatever, little big brother." TK and Henry began to laugh.

" My sister is crazy as fuck. Roll a blunt. You take one bag of this shit and I'll take the other. Shit, I'm going to try to get this shit off tomorrow."

Chapter Thirteen

Damn!

Chris had been avoiding Mercedes and didn't want anything to do with her. Mercedes really needed to talk to him and decided to go by his house. Mercedes got out her car and rang the doorbell.

" Hi, my name is Mercedes. Is Chris here?"

" Umm, yes. Wait one moment let me get him. I'm his mom, terry." terry extended her hand to shake Mercedes.

" Nice to meet you I'm his girlfriend." terry looked shocked.

" Oh, I didn't know, he never mentioned you. Let me get him." she closed the door and Mercedes heard her yell, "Chris, get out here." Chris came to the door and was very surprised to see Mercedes.

" What's up Chris?" Mercedes said with her hand on her hip.

" Man, what's up?" Chris replied.

" You tell me what's up. I've been calling you."

" And? I'm cool on you, I moved on."

" When were you going to tell me?"

" I'm telling you now, shit."

" Wow Chris, we been through a lot and you took my virginity. You not just about to leave me like that."

" Girl, gone." Chris tried to close the door and Mercedes put her foot in the way. "Girl move."

" Chris I'm fucking pregnant!" Mercedes eyes filled with tears. "Nice to know what type of father my child is going to have. Piece of shit", she moved her foot and walked down the stairs.

Chris didn't know terry was standing behind him listening to the conversation.

"Boy, go get her now." terry said in anger. Chris ran behind her.

" Hey, wait." Chris said as he grabbed her arm. "Come in the house so we can sit down and talk." Mercedes followed him inside the house and they sat on the coach.

" Why didn't you tell me?" Chris yelled.

" Chris I been calling you and you never answer the phone." Terry walked in and handed Mercedes a glass of water.

" How old are you baby?" Terry asked.

" 16."

" Awww, you poor thing. Did you tell your mom?"

" No. I thought I'd tell the father first to decide what to do." she gave Chris an evil eye and he bowed his head in shame. "I'm not keeping it."

" What? When did you decide this?" Chris screamed.

" Man, Chris please. I decided this when I found out and called to tell you and you were dogging me."

" I am so sorry. I really am." Chris walked over to Mercedes and put his arms around her. "I want to be the father, and I promise to be a good father, just give me a chance."

" This ain't not game Chris, it's a life. You're not going to be able to just walk in and out on this child when you feel like it or when you feel things are getting hard."

" I know, cedes. I promise to always be there for our baby and you." he kissed her on the lips. "I love you."

" How do you know it's his?" terry asked. Mercedes looked at her with her face frowned.

" I'm not a hoe, he's the only one I been with. I'm not about to explain myself to anyone. When the baby come, take a DNA test. When you see the results, pick your fucking face up off the floor." Mercedes grabbed her purse and headed towards the door.

" Mama! It's mines. She ain't like that." he followed behind Mercedes and walked her to her car.

" What do you think your mom is going to say? Chris asked.

" I don't know. I know she'll be upset. Shit she had me at this age."

" I know, do you want me to be there with you when you tell her?"

" You'll do that?"

" Yes, I love you." Mercedes smiled.

" Naw, I need to tell her by myself." Chris kissed her and Mercedes got in the car.

" I'm going to call you later. We're having a baby." Chris smiled. "I'm excited."

" See you later," she replied in a low tone.

Chris walked back in the house and Terry stood at the door. "Sorry Chris, you know I'm supportive in everything you do."

" I know mama."

" I just don't want you throwing you future away."

" I'm not throwing my future away, I'm building it. I'm still going to go to college and get a good job. Besides I'm having a baby now, so I have motivation." Chris walked into his room and closed the door.

Here we go!

When Mercedes walked in the house her mom's car wasn't there. She ran a bubble bath and relaxed. She decided to cook dinner and clean up the house. When Shyann and Lexus walked in the house, she assumed Mercedes wanted something.

" Hey cedes. You cooked and cleaned up? What you want?" Shyann asked.

" Mama, I know you be working hard, so I thought I'd help you out a little more often around here."

" Yeah. I bet."

" Mercedes I went shopping with mama today. Look what I got." showing her a pair of pastry shoes. "You like them?" Lexus asked.

" Yes, their cute. Wash your hands so you can eat." Lexus ran to the bathroom.

"Mama I need to talk to you."

" What's up baby?"

" Mama I'm. . ." Mercedes ran over to the kitchen trashcan and threw up.

" Damn. Girl is you pregnant?" Mercedes shook her head yes. "Man, what the hell. I don't want you following my footsteps. I want you to be better than I was. Fuck Mercedes." Shyann was very upset, she grabbed her keys and left.

" Where is mama going?" Lexus asked.

Relax.

Shyann's phone rang and she looked down to see the caller id, it was JJ. She didn't feel like talking so she pressed ignore. He called back again.

" What?" she snapped.

" Damn, my fault ma. You mad or something?" JJ replied.

" Naw, my fault JJ, what's up?"

" I was just calling to say thanks for showing me love on my b-day and shit. I wanted to know if you could stop by and shit for a minute."

" For what?"

" Just chill with your boy, continue the celebration."

" Shit, sure I need to relax and clear my head for a minute anyways. I'll be there in 10."

" Alright."

Shyann was upset and couldn't believe what Mercedes had done. She wondered was the boy Chris and how she could do something so dumb. Then she said to herself, "damn, I was the same fucking way." she realized that she couldn't be mad at Mercedes. She was about to turn around and go back and apologize to Mercedes but wanted to see JJ, so she sent her a text.

" Hey baby, sorry for over reacting and leaving. I was wrong, I just been in your shoes and I know the walk that your about to face. I love you and I'm here for you. I'll be home soon."

Mercedes read the text and smiled and replied . . ."thanks mom, love you too."

JJ was cheesing as she walked in his apartment. "Hey ma." he hugged her tight.

" What's up?"

" Nothing, I'm chillin'. I got some patron and purple cush and shit." he handed her a zip lock sandwich bag. She smelled it.

" Damn, this smell like some fire!"

" It is, roll up a blunt. Here!" he handed her a grape blunt wrap. Shyann stopped smoking several months ago but the smell of that Cush made her give in. she rolled up a blunt and JJ poured them a shot of patron.

" Damn, that's a fat ass blunt." JJ said joking around.

" If you're going to smoke, smoke right. I don't smoke small ass blunts and shit. You got a lighter nigga?"
JJ handed her a lighter and poured two more shots for them. Shyann hit the blunt and began coughing.

" Damn nigga." they both laughed. "This shit good." she took the other shot of patron down. JJ had intentions and Shyann was very aware of them, she wanted him just as bad as he wanted her. She poured another shot and hit the blunt again. Shyann haven't smoked in a long time so she was high as fuck.

" Here ma." JJ said handing her the blunt. Shyann eyes became blood shot read. She wasn't drunk her alcohol tolerance was high so the three shots did nothing but give her a minor buzz.

" Ok, that's some fire as Cush JJ." she said smiling from cheek to cheek.

"Nigga, guess what!. . .man cedes pregnant."

" For real." Shyann shook her head yes. "Damn, you gonna let her keep it."

" Hell yeah, abortion is not an option. I just wish she how've waited that's all, but that shit is done so what can I do."

" How far alone is she?"

" I don't even know I left when she told me. I'll talk to her about it later. She just so smart though, she get all A's my nigga." JJ just stared at Shyann while she was talking and put the blunt out.

" I'm high as hell ma."

" Shit me too." they both began laughing. "Ain't felt this good in a long time. Come sit over here by me nigga, I ain't going to bite you. But if I do I promise it wont hurt." Shyann giggled. JJ poured another shot of patron and sat next to Shyann.

Shyann put her hand on his dick, which she noticed was hard. "What that shit do nigga?"

JJ began to laugh. "I can't tell you, I have to show you." he smiled and began kissing on her neck. He filled on her big juicy breast and moved his way to her belly button. He pulled her shirt off slowly over her head and removed her bra k. he began slowly and gently sucking on her nipples and with one hand rubbing on her pussy through her jeans. Shyann pulled his Levi's down and his boxes down. She played with his balls with her fingertips.

JJ removed her jeans and g-string and with 2 fingers he played with her pussy. She began to get wet and sucked on his neck. Shyann began to cum as JJ ate her out. She controlled his head and she cummed in his mouth. JJ stood up and took his Jordan's off and pulled his jeans down to his ankles. JJ's dick was fat and looked about 9inches. Shyann didn't know if it was because of the cush or patron, but whatever it was made her want him badly.

" Come here." Shan said sitting up on the coach and JJ stood in front of her.

"You look sweet." Shyann smiled and kissed his dick. She rang her tongue from the tip of his dick to his balls and began sucking them. She began giving him slow blow and making love to his dick with her mouth.

JJ played with her pussy as she sucked his dick. JJ rolled his red eyes in the back of his head and moaned. Shyann began going a little faster and JJ almost fell over. He pulled his dick out her mouth and stood her up and turned her around. Shyann began grinding on his hard dick and he bent her over face down. He inserted his dick into her pussy nice and slow. Shyann was wet; JJ licked his lips and gave her nice and easy pumps. They both moaned.

Shyann tapped JJ. "Move back a little." JJ took a few steps back and Shyann flipped upside down. Her head was on the ground and her legs were in the air. JJ grabbed her ankles and began pumping. JJ pulled out and Shyann sat up on the coach and began sucking his dick. JJ laid her down and turned into the 69 position and began eating her out. He pumped in her mouth and fucked her face. He felt he was about to cum so he turned around and inserted his dick back into her pussy. He went slow and kissed her on the neck.

" I'm about to cum.," he whispered in her ear.

" Me too." she grabbed his back and pulled him closer and tightened up her pussy walls. JJ had never felt anyone do that during sex and it felt good. He began to cum and Shyann pulled tighter and he couldn't resist the feeling and came inside of her. Shyann lay there with her eyes closed and feel asleep.

JJ awoke about 20 minutes later and pulled out of Shyann and her eyes opened. Juices ran out as he pulled out. "Man." Shyann said and smiled.
" That was bomb!" JJ smiled. "Take a shower with me."
" Okay." Shyann poured another shot of patron then went into the bathroom where JJ was running the hot water.
" Here." he handed her a towel.
" This shit clean nigga? I know you always got bitches over," she said smiling.
" Yeah it's clean. I washed it myself with tide." He smiled. "And I don't bring bitches in my house. I go to there's."
" Shut up stupid," they laughed as they got in the shower. JJ took a bar of soap and washed Shyann up. He wiped every part of her body, and then she did his. They both stood under the water and kissed. When they finished they went into his bedroom and he rubbed lotion on Shyann. He massaged her back and admired her beautiful body.

Trash it!
Some girls from the club were breaking into Shyann's shop. Whoever was suppose to lock up that night, didn't set the alarm. The whole store was trashed and racks of clothes had been taken along with shoes. Shyann lay peacefully with JJ and for the first time in a long time had comfort from someone that wasn't paying her. Her cell phone was in the living room so she didn't hear it blowing up.

Chapter Fourteen

A night to remember.
" Good morning beautiful." JJ stood over Shyann as she awoke he was fully dressed.
" Good morning. What time is it?"
JJ looked at his guess watch and answered. "10:15am."
" Fuck! Why didn't you wake me up nigga?" Shyann yelled hopping out the bed to put her clothes on.
" My bad ma, you looked tired." he followed behind her walking towards the living room.
" It's cool, I got to go." Shyann reached in her purse for her phone and saw 31 missed calls. Mercedes had been calling her along with silver (the alarm company). Her heart began to beat really fast so she sat down and called Mercedes back.

" What happened?" Shyann asked.
" Mama, somebody broke into the store last night. I been trying to call you, the alarm company called all last night. I'm at the store now with grandma and Lexus. Where are you?"
" Damn, I'm on my way." Shyann grabbed her keys and headed towards the door. JJ knew from the look on her face that something was wrong.

" What's up ma?"
" Someone broke into my fucking store. I'm here fucking around with your ass and look what happens. Fuck!" Shyann snapped.
" Awww, shit. Sorry to hear that ma!" JJ wanted to argue with her and say it wasn't his fault but he saw how hurt and upset she was so he let it go and killed her with kindness. "Here, let me go with you." JJ grabbed his keys and followed Shyann to her truck and got in.
" You don't have to go if you don't want too."
" I know, but I want too. That's the least I can do, since you were with me all night!" he replied being a smartass.
" I didn't mean it like that!"

" And I didn't take it like that!" JJ smiled. He really liked Shyann and wanted to be there for her. "I'm about to make some phone calls and see who heard something about it right now."
Shyann smiled. "Thanks, I'm going to fucking kill whoever did this shit."

They arrived at the store and got out. Shyann couldn't believe her eyes.
"Mama!" Mercedes yelled.
" Do you know who did this?" Shyann asked the officer.
" No, but, some people across the street saw 2 people running from the scene, a block that way, (he pointed to the right) and called the police. Were going to need you to come down and make a police report. We'll try our best to find out who was responsible."
" Thanks." JJ walked up beside Shyann and Mercedes smiled.
" Hi, JJ." she said giving him a hug.
" Hey, what's up? Hey, Megan and Lexus." they both smiled and waved.

" What are you going to do child?" Megan asked Shyann.
" Start over again, fuck them. They aint stopping shit, and when I find out who did this shit, there died."
" Stop talking that stupidness girl. Let god deal with them, you just start over."
" Yea, mama." Shyann walked inside the store to see the mess. JJ began picking up clothes and trash.
" You got a broom, ma?" JJ asked.
" Ummm, yeah but, you ain't got to clean up. I'll hire some people to come in tomorrow."
" You sure, because you know I got you."
" Yes I'm sure." Shyann smiled. "You got me?" Shyann walked over to JJ and stood face to face.
" Yup ma', I got you. Real shit." JJ began to laugh. "Ma, your breath stank." they both began laughing.
" Awwww, you're wrong for that one." JJ grabbed her and pulled her closer.

" I aint trippin' though." he kissed her on the lips.

" Mama!" Lexus screamed.
" Yes baby."
" I'm hungry, Mercedes didn't fix me breakfast."
" Ok baby, let's all go to ihop."
" Ok." Lexus smiled and ran to tell Mercedes and Megan. Shyann and JJ walked back out to the curb where they were standing. The glass front door had been broken and shattered. It looks like whoever did it, broke it just enough to reach through and unlock it. Shyann had JJ board the door with wood from the inside while she pulled the curtains closed and set the alarm.
" Who was supposed to set the alarm Mercedes?" Mercedes put her head down.
" Me. I am so sorry mama."
" Ok, it's cool. Let's go." Shyann wanted to say more but felt it was no reason. What's done is done, and if anyone is to blame it's Shyann. It's her store and she left a teenager in charge.
" I'm riding with you." Lexus said to Shyann, running towards the truck. Megan couldn't believe how calm Shyann was, she was very surprised. Megan rode in the car with Mercedes and they followed Shyann to the restaurant.

" Your mama is very calm for some reason." Megan said.
" Maybe her new boyfriend." Mercedes giggled.
" JJ! Please. Shy better leave him alone.
" I like him, he's cool . . . grandma, I don't know if mama told you or not but, I'm pregnant."
Megan was shocked. "What?" she snapped. "You damn kids are something else. You want to be just like your mother?"
" Just like my mother? What does that mean?"
" Nothing child, throw your life away."
" Mama, did it and made it . . ." Megan cut her off.
" So you think you can, huh?"
" Think, no! I know I can, mama got her degree and everything."

" Yeah, it took her a long time too." Mercedes couldn't believe what she was hearing. She thought her grandmother would be a little more supportive.

" I'm going to be a good mother to my child, that's all I can say. Watch!"

" You need to finish school and go to college and." Mercedes cut her off.

" Grandma, no disrespect but, I am and I will and when I do, don't congratulate me please." Megan just shook her head; she wanted more for Mercedes just as she did for Shyann when she had Mercedes. "Imagine if my mama would've had an abortion with me, wow. I wouldn't be here!"

" Cedes, I'm sorry. I didn't mean it like that I love you. You and your sister and I wouldn't trade you guys for the world, I just want the best for you that's all."

" Yeah granny, I want the best for me too." they drove the rest of the ride in silence and Mercedes turned her face as tears rolled down.

" How many?" the host asked.

" 5." Shyann replied. She noticed Mercedes looked like she was crying as they walked to their seat. "What's wrong cedes?"

" Nothing, I need to go to the bathroom."

" Me too." Lexus said. Mercedes grabbed her hand and they walked to the bathroom.

" Mama, what's wrong with Cedes? I asked and she said nothing, I know she lying."

" She told me she was pregnant and I told her she throwing her life away." Megan snapped.

" Mama, what's done is done! Don't loose your grandchild over a mistake she made. You know what I don't even want to have this conversation. I'm sure your response was the same when I told you."

" Like mother, like daughter." Megan pulled her purse closer to her.

" Mama, please don't start!" Shyann said looking at the menu. JJ just sat there quiet, texting on his phone. Mercedes and Lexus sat down at the table.

" I want some pancakes." Lexus said smiling. They all ordered their food and ate. Everyone talked but Megan, she ate in silence and short answered all questions that she was asked. Shyann reached in her purse to get her wallet and pay the bill.

" I got it ma." JJ said.

" I got it too."

" Let me pay, damn!" JJ snapped. "That's what a man does for his woman." Shyann laughed.

" Your not my man JJ."

" I am, you just don't know it yet." he smiled.

" Yeah, Ok! Pay so we can go." JJ paid the bill and tipped the waitress $50.

Chapter Fifth-Teen

Going back.

Shyann hung out with JJ for the next few days. She hadn't talked to Henry and Megan and Mercedes weren't talking. She couldn't accept the fact that she wasn't making money daily anymore so went back to work at Tasty's. She spoke with her financial evaluator and Shyann decided to remodel the whole store and build an upstairs. He told her it'll be a little pricey, but he'll try to get the best people in town to quote it and he'll get back to her

" Ben, baby. I'm coming back."

" Star, it's been a lot of talk about you up here. i don't want no problems from you."

" Talk? What kind of talk?"

" Someone thinks you had something to do with, what happened to Tish."

" Man, I don't know what you talking about." Stacy popped in here mind.

" Star I don't need no bullshit up here."

" Ben! You know me better than that."

" That's exactly why I said what I said. Go on and get dressed star, half these damn niggas in here for you anyways shit."

" Thanks, Ben." Star kissed him on the cheek. Star saw Stacy and wanted to snap that bitch neck, but she had something up here sleeve so she gave her a pass.

" Star baby." Stacy had gotten thin since the last time star saw in without clothes. Her face looked sucked in and you could see her bones poking out her skin. She looked like she had started using. Star knew it had to have been Stacy popping off at the fucking mouth.

" What's up ma?" Star said without eye contact.

" I missed you!" she smiled.

" I'm sure you did ma, I'm back now, so get use to seeing me around more." Star changed her clothes and put her things in the locker.

" Oh, ok. That's what's up." Meeka and Bree walked up to Stacy.

" Stacy, we got some shit come check it out. What's up Star, sorry about what happened to your store. That's was fucked up, looks like your back here with the rest of us, huh?" Bree said and Stacy looked at Star.

" What happened to your store? I was just there a few days ago." She asked.

" Someone broke into my shit, they dumb asses didn't know I had cameras on the outside." She looked at Meeka and Bree, lying threw her teeth, but wanted to see how they'd react. They had guilty written all over their faces.

" Fo'real?" Meeka snapped, Bree gave her a look, like shut the fuck up!

" Yeah, but I ain't trippin'. It take more than that to tare me down. I'm rebuilding and restocking." She turned to look Bree in the eyes. "Who told you my store got broken into?" Bree froze and hesitated to answer, star waited a few seconds for a reply, but got nothing. "I thought so!" star closed her locker and walked away.

Star did her usual, put the hating ass bitches behind her and made her money. With all that she was going through with the sore and her family, she had a lot on her mind. She wanted to kill them bitches but knew she had being doing a lot lately and needed to slow down. James was sitting in the corner watching Star, when she noticed she walked over to him.

" Hey, baby!"
" Sit down." He snapped.
" What's up?" She said smiling.
" I found these photos under my mattress." He showed her the photos of them together.
" Why you showing me this shit?" She snapped.
" Man, are you that dumb? Somebody took these of us, which means, somebody was watching us. My fucking wife is dead! Someone killed her and I need to find out who did it."

" Damn, I'm sorry to hear that. I didn't know." She was shocked and hopped he didn't put his nose in it too much and try to figure it out. She didn't want to kill him, but she would if she had too. She played along and showed sympathy.

" I don't think she was killed, the police said her car over heated and caught on fire or something like that, I saw it on the news. I didn't know that was your wife, why didn't you tell me?"

" The police are liars, that's what they said but the story sounds funny to me. I think she was cheating and whoever she was messing with... maybe she was suppose to leave me and she didn't and he killed her." Star smiled inside and thought that was a good story to run with.

" You know what, that does make sense. Man, that's crazy, he probably wanted money or something."

" I need to ask you, have you seen anyone following you or anything strange? Because right here. ." He handed her a photo of her parking her truck in the parking lot at Tasty's. "They took a picture of you."

" Oh." Her mouth opened with shock. She pretended she didn't know anything about someone following her. "Sorry about your wife, I have kids so I hope that person didn't follow me home and know where I leave."

" Me too, sorry for putting you in my bull shit."

" It's cool." She kissed him on the cheek. "Thanks for the warning."

Chapter Sixteen

A lot of stress.

School had started back and Mercedes just hit 3 months. Her and Chis were doing well and were really excited about the baby. Mercedes and Shyann agreed that she could go first semester, have home schooling for the second semester, then go back to school her senior year. This was Chris' last year and he wanted to focus on graduation. Mercedes couldn't cheer lead this year and was a little down it. Mercedes and Chris walked down the hallway.

" Hey Chris." Porsha said.
" What's up?" Mercedes replied with an attitude. Porsha was Chris' ex-girlfriend.
" What's up?" Chris said, grabbing Mercedes hand.
" I heard you were having a baby and want to say good luck, that's all." she smiled and walked away.
" What was that all about?" Mercedes asked.
" That bitch just jealous." Chris replied and walked Mercedes to her class. "I'll catch you later, love you." he kissed her on the forehead and walked away.
" Love you too. Hey!" Chris turned back around. "You still going to the doctor with me after school.
" Awww, shit, I have practice. What time is the appointment?"
" It's at 4, don't trip I'll have Lexus ride with me."
" Okay, thanks for understanding. I'll go to the next one, I promise."
" Yeah." Mercedes really wanted him to go with her she wanted his support.

After school Mercedes walked on the football field to see Chris before she left. She saw him talking to Porsha and her whole attitude changed. She walked up and they were giggling. Chris was surprised to see Mercedes when he noticed her standing behind Porsha.
" What's so funny?" Mercedes snapped. "Why this bitch all up in your face Chris?"

" Bitch? I got your bitch." Porsha replied. Chris stood in the middle of them.

" Man, chill we were just talking." He said to Mercedes and turned to look at Porsha. "Look I'll see you later."

" Yeah, fa'sho. Tell your bitch to watch her back." Porsha rolled her eyes at Mercedes and walked away.

" You always starting shit."

" Nigga, please! What did I start? Your the one over here giggling and laughing with the next hoe."

" It wasn't even like that!"

" I'm sure it wasn't. You keep in mind who's having your child Chris."

" Here you go, what the fuck that got to do with anything?"

" It has a lot because I will beat the shit out of her and not think twice about it. So keep the bull shit and stress to yourself because I don't have time for your hoe ass."

" I ain't no hoe, but anyways stop trippin'. I have to get back to practice we got a game on Friday and some colleges are coming to watch me play."

" Oh, so you're going to go off to school. What about me and the baby."

" Look Cedes, damn! I'll be local; I'm not going out of State anymore. You and the baby will be fine."

" Yeah, whatever Chris. You're so full of shit. I have to go, maybe I'll call you after my appointment."

Mercedes went to pick up Lexus early from the after school program and went to her doctor's appointment. She realized she snapped and wanted to text Chris and apologize, but she let her pride get the best of her and didn't. She thought he was being selfish for going to college but realized she was the one being selfish. She began crying.

" What's wrong Cedes?" Lexus asked.

" Nothing, you wouldn't understand."

" How would you know, if you don't give me a chance to understand." Mercedes smiled.

" That's true huh? I'm okay, the pregnancy just makes me emotional sometimes and I cry for no reason."

" Oh, that sucks. I hope when I get bigger that don't happen to me. When kids cry at school the other kids laugh."

" It's kind of different being older, but you'll see when it's your turn."

" See I told you I could understand." Lexus put her hand on her shoulder.

"You'll be okay." Mercedes smiled at her little sister; she made her feel better too.

When they got back in from the doctor, Shyann's car wasn't there so Mercedes called her to tell her what the doctor said.

" Hey mama."

" Hey baby, how was school? What Lexus doing?"

" It was good, Chris ex-girlfriend is getting on my nerves, but it's whatever. Lexus doing the rest of her homework, I took her to the doctor with me. The baby due on March 21st." she said smiling.

" That's good."

" I want to know what it is but she said I'm not far alone to tell."

" Yeah, it has to be like 5 months I believe. But that's good, did yall eat?"

" I bought your daughter some McDonald's so you owe me some money. I'm not hungry, I'm kind of sleepy."

" Well get some rest, don't let this baby pull your grades down, do your homework."

" I will mama. See you when you get here. Love you."

" Love you too, kiss Lexus for me I'll be there shortly."

" Okay." she hung up the phone.

Chapter Seventeen

Here we go.

Shyann and JJ had been spending a lot of time together. Shyann knew it was wrong but it felt so right. She knew if Nate found out that he would be upset, all she was thinking about was her happiness.

" JJ, I'm about to go."

" Where you going to shake your ass at that club. Man, the homies said they seen you in there. How you think that makes me feel?. . My homies can see my girl half naked and shit."

" Pump ya' breaks nigga. I ain't ya' fucking girl and you knew my get down before we started fucking."

" Oh, you ain't my girl? What you call it then, because I just don't be spending time and money on females."

" Wow, okay!. . .you really want to go there with me! Nigga we ain't together, and how yo' dumb ass act, won't be any time soon either. I'm not your bitch and you're not my nigga. We fuck, we smoke, we drink, we chill, we buy each other shit from time to time, that's it! Take it how it is nigga and nothing more."

" You got me fucked up!"

" Naw, reality of the situation is, you got yourself fucked up! I'm out, don't worry about calling me Jonathan Jones!"

" Bye, Shyann Thomas. Saying my whole name and shit like I care."
Shyann slammed the front door and left.
Shyann started back smoking Cush, she'd smoke about 3 times and day and quickly picked up her nasty habit again. When Shyann smoked she felt relaxed, free and calm. Shyann sat in the car and rolled a blunt really quickly and drove off.

Her phone rang and it was JJ, she pressed ignore. He called back again.

" What!" she snapped.

" Look man, I'm sorry okay. We've been friends for a long ass time and we look out for each other. I don't want to fuck that up. I'm sorry. Do you forgive me?"

" I been over it, so it is what it is."

" Man, what the fuck does that mean? I said I'm sorry, I expected you to say, I forgive you or something. Not no bull shit like that."
" You know what, your about to blow my high! I forgive you JJ, I have to go home and cook dinner for my kids."
" Alright, ma! Can I call you later?"
" Yeah, whatever bye." Shyann hung the phone up.

Shyann got home and checked on the girls, they both were doing their homework.
" Hey."
" Mama." Lexus screamed when she saw her mom standing at the den door.
" Hey mama." Mercedes said. "Were just doing our homework."
" I'm almost done mama." Lexus said.
" Okay, that's good. I'm going to take a quick shower and cook some spaghetti." Shyann said.
" Oh, yes." Lexus said smiling. Mercedes smiled at her funny little dance she did with her arms.
" Girl you so silly." Shyann smiled and walked into her bedroom. Mercedes came in behind her.
" Mama, I want to go see daddy. In his letter he said he wanted to see me and I want to tell him in person I'm having a baby."
" Ummm, okay baby. I'm not going to tell you, you can't see your father. Things between him and I are not the best right now."
" I know, he told me, but I think we all should go see him, please."
" Sure. We'll go this weekend." Shyann didn't want to see Nate, but she didn't want to keep the kids from him so she decided to go.

Chapter Eighteen

Visiting Nate Blake.

Shyann and the girls got up early Saturday morning to go visit Nate at Avenal state prison. Shyann didn't want to see Nate; she'd falling out of love and felt betrayed. She really wished he wasn't in the situation that he was in and was upset because she couldn't do anything about it.

" Wake up guys, we're here!" Shyann said. Mercedes face lite up with a big smile. Lexus wasn't as excited, she didn't know her father very well, and the memories of him that she had were a blur.

" Man, I can't wait to see him." Mercedes said excited. Shyann's phone rings.

" Hello!"

" Hey, ma! You made it?" JJ asked.

" Yeah, we just pulled up now, I'm just looking for parking." Shyann replied.

" Oh, okay. Well tell that nigga I said what's up. Call me when you leave."

" Alright." Shyann hung up the phone.

" I'm telling daddy about your new boy friend." Lexus said in a joking tone.

" You ain't going to say shit!" Lexus jumped back as if her feelings were hurt. "Our business is our business, got that? Your father has way more to worry about than what I'm doing."

" Okay." Lexus said in a sad tone.

" You don't need to be snapping at her because you're mad at daddy. Come on Lexus." Mercedes grabbed her hand and walked towards the line.

" Girl, I will kick your ass up and down this parking lot." Shyann snapped.

" Yeah!" Mercedes rolled her eyes. "Come on mama."

" I'm coming, stop rushing me shit!"

They entered the visiting room and the bailiff told them to have a seat and wait. Mercedes saw Nate walking from the back and stood up with a smile on her face.

" Daddy!" she waived. Nate smiled. They sat down at the table and Nate walked over and hugged everyone.

" I miss you so much!" he held Shyann tight and whispered in her ear. "I know I fucked up but I love you and need you more than ever right now." Nate eyes filled with water and he kissed her on the neck. Shyann loved Nate but wasn't in love with him anymore, but when he hugged her she felt complete.

" I love you Nate, and I always will." Shyann smiled. He hugged the girls and they sat down.

" Daddy you need a hair cut." Lexus giggled. Nate rubbed his head and smiled.

" Daddy I have something to tell you." Mercedes smiled.

" Yeah, she is having a baby!" Lexus shouted.

" Mama, tell her to shut up. I wanted to tell him myself!" Mercedes snapped at Lexus and pushed her.

" Mama!" Lexus yelled.

" Alright, that's enough." Nate said. "Wow, I'm shocked."

" What does that mean?" Mercedes said, as she frowned her face.

" I'm happy for you but I wish you would've waited."

" Wow, you're one to talk and mama was 16."

" Fuck! Shut up, shut up. We didn't come out here to argue." Shyann snapped.

" Well, what the fuck you doing? Maybe you should be home with them more instead of shaking your ass all night." Nate said. Shyann couldn't believe he said that, he really pissed her off.

" Okay!" she gave a slight laugh. "The motha fucka behind bars, that can't take care of his family got something to say? Nate fuck you, my kids don't go without shit. Fuck you. I'm sorry I ain't a nothing ass mother that doesn't need a man to take care of me and my damn kids!"

" Our kids, our kids, or did you forget I'm their father. Maybe you did because you never bring them to see me, I write your ass and you don't write back."

" Nate, fuck you, you and your bitch that be up here visiting you. That's why I don't bring my kids to come see you." Lexus and Mercedes had blank looks on their faces and Mercedes eyes began to fill with tears. Mercedes thought Nate would be happy for her and be proud to be a grandfather.

" Can yall please stop it!" Mercedes yelled. Everyone in the visiting room stared at them.

" I want to leave mama." Lexus said.

" See your own fucking kids don't even want to be around you!" Nate wanted to grab her by the neck and chock the shit out of her.

" I'm sorry baby." Nate said to Lexus. "Mercedes I'm happy for you, just disappointed in your mother that's all. I love you girls. I wish I could come home with you guys but daddy can't right now. I just need you guys to understand the situation I'm in, that may cause me to over react on situations I have no control over."

" I'm old enough to understand. I was really happy to tell you, you were going to be a grandfather. I'm nothing like my mother!" Mercedes got up and walked out.

" Mercedes!" Nate called. " Come back."

" Damn!"

" Damn." Shyann said grabbing Lexus by the hand. "I have to go get her. Nate you loss your life to the streets already don't loose your kids because you can't control your temper."

" Shyann shut the fuck up, you always got some shit to say. The homies keep me up on game on your hoe ass. You fucking JJ and out there running wild and shit, you worry about loosing your kids!" Nate stood up. "Lexus I love you and I'm sorry. Tell your sister I love her and I'm going to call her tonight." he kissed her on the forehead. Shyann stood there rolling her eyes in disgust and wanted to fire on Nate.

" We have to go!"

" Man fuck you, I'm going to have my mama pick them up next weekend to come visit me without your stupid ass." Nate snapped.

" Yeah, we'll see. You the stupid ass locked up and shit. Fuck you, don't drop the soap nigga!" Shyann grabbed Lexus and left.

Nate couldn't believe what happened and how fast it happened. "Fuck!" he said to his self.

Shyann regrets coming to visit him. Mercedes waited by the car with her arms folded, crying.

" I'm sorry mama!" Mercedes gave her a hug. "I was really upset."

" Baby I know, I'm not trippin! I'm sorry you didn't get the reaction you wanted from your dad."

" I just wanted him to be happy."

" I know, let's go home."

Problem after problem.

When they got back to l.a. Mercedes went to Chris house, she tried calling but his phone was off. She figured it was dead, she just wanted comfort and to be held. She parked in front of the house and got out and knocked on the door.

" Coming." Chris yelled through the door. When he opened the door his face fell to the ground. "Hey." he cleared his throat.

" You busy?" Mercedes asked.

" Ummm, a little. What's up?"

" I just need to talk, I just went to see my dad and. . ." Mercedes stopped, as her eyes grew big. "Damn! Like that?" Porsha walked up behind him. Chris turned and saw her standing there and put his head down.

" Ummm. . .I can explain." Chris said.

" No need." Mercedes pushed the door open and walked in. "Bitch what's up? You're going to keep stepping on my toes huh?"

" Bitch, what are you talking about?" Porsha put her hand in Mercedes face and Mercedes blew up. Mercedes pushed her and Chris stood in between them.

" Not in my house." Chris yelled." Mercedes leave!" Mercedes looked at him in shock.

" Leave? Your going to kick me out over this bitch Chris?

" Man, get the hell out. I don't have time for this."

" You don't have time to deal with the problem but you have time to create the problem. If you haven't noticed I'm pregnant, if you don't want to fuck with me, say that!" Mercedes yelled.

" I'm cool."

" What?"

" I said I'm cool, ever since you found out you were pregnant you been acting like you control me."

" Nigga, you never not once said we weren't together. What the fuck are you talking about? You trying to play rolls in front of this bitch and shit, keep shit real Chris."

" Man, leave." Chris stood in her face.

" Sure!" Mercedes balled her fist up and socked him in the nose. Chris wanted to hit her back, but knew she wasn't worth it. Mercedes walked to her car and cried. Porsha stood there with a slight smile on her face. Chris turned and stared at her.

" Bitch, you can bounce too."

" What?" Porsha snapped.

" You heard me, get your shit and bounce. I hit, that's pretty much all I wanted. Leave!"

" I got your bitch!" Porsha grabbed her things and left.

Chris didn't give a fuck about no bitch, he was stressing from the SAT's and colleges and took it out on whoever he could. He knew he was wrong for doing Mercedes like that but did it anyways.

Stress free, please!

Mercedes couldn't understand what happened and wanted to just get away. She got into it with her grandmother over the baby, her daddy and now Chris. She began to have second thoughts about the baby and was beginning to stress out. She went to one of her best friends house to talk. Mia was a good listener unlike some of Mercedes other friends.

She felt like having the baby was a bad idea and wanted to get an abortion. She just wanted all the problems to go away and be stress free.

" What are you going to do?" Mia asked.

" I don't know, I'm tired and I'm too young for this."

" Girl, I know how you feel. Age has nothing to do with it. Shit we probably go threw more than adults. Pray, it really helps, believe me."

" God has so many people to listen to, he doesn't have time for me."

" Stop it, he has time, as long as you have time for him. I'm not going to encourage you to get an abortion but here are a few clinics if you do decide too." she handed her some papers. "You hungry?"

" Naw, I'm cool. I just have a lot on my mind."

Everything in Shyann's life was getting crazy and she didn't want to deal with it anymore. She hadn't talked to her brother, Nate had completely blown up on her, and she worried about the store and how she was going to handle the bitches that were behind it. Every time she talked to JJ, they argued, she became very unhappy within the last two weeks.

She thought, what do you do when you no longer feel in control of your life? She rolled a Cush blunt and smoked it while taking a nice long hot bubble bath.

Chapter Nineteen

Take them out.

Shyann and JJ was chillin at his house smoking and drinking. Shyann began smoking everyday again, and had began to loose focus fucking around with JJ. JJ loved Shyann and the feelings he had for her grew stronger over the last few months.

" I found out who fucked up my shop."

" For real?"

" Yeah, two bitches I work with. Meeka and Bree bitch asses. I knew but just been deciding how to deal with them."

" I feel you, you need to be cool though. You be moving to fast and shit."

" What that mean?"

" Man you know, but I got your back. You know that, but if I'm in were going to do it right and smooth."

" Is that right?" Shyann smiled.

" Yup! Your my baby, I love your ass always have."

" I love you too. Nate knows about us."

" I know!"

" Damn, why didn't you tell me?"

" Shit, I thought you knew. I don't give a fuck; I respect that nigga to the fullest. If I was him, I'd rather you be with me, than these other niggas out here."

" I have been thinking about moving to Atlanta."

" Damn, fo'real?"

" Yeah."

" Fo'real, for how long now?"

" A few weeks."

" Damn, so just up and leave everyone."

" I was hoping you come too."

" Naw. Well I'm not going to say no, but this is where I make my paper."

" I know you got stacks and I got stacks too, we can open our own business and live right."

" I'm not going to say yes, or no, but I'll think about it. When you trying to do this?"
" Some time next year."
" We'll see what's up." JJ smiled and kissed her.
" Okay. I work on Wednesday I want to get them bitches."
" What did you have in mind?"
" I don't know." They both began laughing. "I plan shit as I go, because every time I pan shit, it goes wrong."
" You know what, don't trip. I'll come up there with the homies and take care of them for you."

Shyann cell phone rings.
" Hello!"
" Hey."
" What's up Henry?"
" Shit, I just wanted to see what you were up to and shit. You good?"
" Yeah, I'm straight. How about yourself?"
" I'm cool, I guess. I need some cash."
" Man, I haven't heard from you and you're asking for money."
" Shy I'll pay you back. You going to give it to me or not?"
" Man, you know I got you. How much you need? TK told me yall split that cheese 2 ways that night. You always fucking over me, but it's cool. You always need me before I need you."
" Man, yo' ass left, you got over on yourself. I need 10,000$."
" What the fuck ever. This is my last time helping you. Come to the house in the morning and I'll give it to you."
" Thanks Shy."
" Bye, Henry!"

Shyann noticed Mercedes been quiet for the last couple of days. They haven't really talked since they saw Nate. She figured she'd just give her, her space. Mercedes was in her bedroom lying on the bed.
" Knock, knock! Can I come in?" Shyann asked.

" Yes mama. Even if I say no, you'll still come in anyways," she giggled. "I went by grandma's today and talked to her."

" Oh, that was mature of you."

" Yeah, I'm not keeping the baby mama."

" Did your grandmother talk you into that?" Shyann snapped.

" No, mama. She actually tried to convince me to keep it. But this is too stressful for me."

" I don't believe in abortions, I want you to make your own mistakes in life, but if I had an abortion with you, you wouldn't be here. Think about it long and hard, pray about it as well."

Tears rolled down her face. "Chris is with Porsha and he dogged me when I went over there." she began telling her what happened, and started crying.

" Baby, it'll be okay." Shyann embraced her with a long hug.

" Daddy hates me and Chris hates me too."

" I love you! They care about you too, men just have a hard time with showing it."

" I just need some time to think and clear my mind. Can you check me out of school and into home school please?"

" No problem, I'll do it tomorrow. Look, I've been thinking about moving to Atlanta, how would you feel about that?"

" Right now, I wouldn't mind at all." Shyann understood how cedes was feeling.

Wednesday night.

Shyann went to work, as usual but wasn't feeling the same. She texted JJ and told him not to come tonight.

He replied. "Why?"

" I got so much on my mind, tonight isn't the right night. Thanks though, we'll handle those hoes another time."

" Alright, if you say so ma. If you change your mind, hit me up."

" Okay."

" What's up Star baby!" Stacy approached her.

" Hey."

" Hey I need to tell you something, I been chilling with Meeka and Bree and…"

" And what?" Star rudely snapped.

" I think they had something to do with your store," she whispered.

" Oh, how you no?"

" They were giggling and laughing about it, and Bree made a little smart comment. I mean, I'm not for sure, for sure, but my gut telling me I'm right."

" Well thanks for telling me." Star closed her locker.

" You seem different lately."

" Naw ma, you the one different." star put her hand under her nose and moved it from right to left. "They fucking turning you out just like everyone else in this bitch. Didn't your mother ever tell you, don't go to the deep end of the pool if you can't swim?"

" I work better when I'm. . ."

Star cut her off and smiled an evil smile folding her arms. "High off coke? Sad!" Star walked away. Stacy stood there staring in the mirror. She didn't recognize who she was and what she was doing. Bree walked up.

" Hey, girl. Hello are you there?" Bree waived her hand in front of her face.

" Yeah, I'm here. Wha-what's up?" She had blacked out for a second.

" What the hell is wrong with you? I got some shit. Come in the back with me and Meeka."

" Okay." Stacy went in the back and they sniffed their coke.

Chapter Twenty

I'm ready!

Mercedes drove to downtown L.A. and cried the whole ride. She had an appointment at 9am. She dropped Lexus off at school and told her mom she was going to the School to clear out her locker. Chris had been calling her and she had been ignoring his calls. When he calls the house she would have Lexus or Shyann answer and say she wasn't in.

She pulled into the parking lot and saw people holding signs and yelling. She had never been to an abortion clinic so she didn't expect it would be protesters. They were yelling, "murderers!" a lady stopped her and handed her a flyer.

" Don't do it, don't do it!"

" Can you get out of my face." She pushed the lady and walked passed her.

" The baby wants to live." She yelled as Mercedes walked in the clinic.

" Hi, I have an appointment for 9am."

" What's your name?" The lady at the front desk asked.

" Mercedes Blake."

" Okay, fill out these papers and bring them up when you're done."

" Okay." Mercedes began filling out the paper work. The girl across from her smiled and she smiled back.

" I'm Kaygin."

" Hi, I'm Mercedes. How far along are you?"

" I look big huh?" she smiled. "I'm 19 weeks."

" Wow."

" And you?"

" 13 1/2."

" Awwww, are you excited?"

" I was, but not any more."

" This is my first baby, I'm really excited." Kaygin said smiling.

" Your excited to kill your baby?"

" No, why would I do that? Oh, you think I'm here for an abortion? My sister work here and she forgot her keys, I just came to drop them off. She's with a patient so I'm just waiting. You're going to go through with the abortion?"

" Yeah, I came all this way."

" I bet if you were that baby, you would want a chance at life. Think about it."

" Kaygin!" her sister called from the front desk.

" I have to go, kids are blessing, don't miss out on yours because the blessing didn't come how you wanted it. All that matters is that it came. Just think about all the people out here who can't have kids and would love to have them." she smiled and got up. "Take care and I wish you the best."

Mercedes closed her eyes and zoned out!

Think twice.

" Mama." a little girl said. "Mama."

" Yes, baby."

" Come get me."

" Where are you? I can't see you."

" Here mama! Help. I'm trapped," she cried.

" I can't see you baby." She ran down a long black hallway. "Where are you?"

" Hurry. I need you," she whispered.

Mercedes began sweating really bad. "Where are you? You have to speak up, your whispering, I can't hear."

" I'm right here. Look. Mama sometimes whispering is the best way to get someone's attention."

" Where am I?" Mercedes was trapped in a very small room that was very dark.

" Help me, I'm right here?" The little girl whispered again.

" Where baby?" she found the light switch on the wall and flicked it up. Light covered the tiny room and the walls were covered with mirrors.

" Right here!" she felt wind cross her stomach as if someone ran by quickly. She looked in the mirror and saw her belly round and big. She was nine months and felt a kick. She looked in the mirror and rubbed her belly. Tears ran down her face, as she stood there naked.

" Baby?"

Mercedes snapped back to reality and hopped up. The clipboard and papers fell to the ground. She quickly picked them up and placed them in the chair and left. She ran out and through the crowd and went to her car. She put her head on the steering wheel and cried.

" What am I doing?" She cried aloud to herself. She reached in her purse for her cell phone.

" Mama!"
" Mercedes, what's wrong?" Shyann could tell in her tone that she was crying.
" I can't kill the baby."
" Mercedes where are you? Stay there I'm on my way."
" I don't know what to do. I'm downtown at the abortion clinic."
" Baby, I'm on the way. Sit tight. What happened?" Shyann got in her truck and drove to where Mercedes was. She stayed on the phone with her the whole time til she pulled in the parking lot.
" Okay baby, I'm here!" She got out of the truck and got in Mercedes car and sat in the passenger seat. Mercedes hugged her tight.
" I am so sorry!" She cried. "I couldn't do it mama."
" It's okay baby."
When Shyann found out the was pregnant with Mercedes she didn't plan to keep her. She made an appointment to get an abortion at 2months. Shyann had a vision just like Mercedes did and couldn't go threw with it. It was like Mercedes was begging her not to kill her. Shyann cried with Mercedes and held her tight.
" I completely understand how you feel baby. It's okay let it out. Mommy is here for you."

Mercedes woke up after sleeping for a few hours and went into the living room with Shyann. Shyann was lying on the couch watching television on her 72" Plasma flat screen.
" Hey."
" Hey baby, how are you feeling?" Shyann asked.

" I'm okay. I'm just so confused Mama!" Tears rolled down her face.

" It's okay. That baby is a blessing from God, and only he can take it away."

" Chris doesn't even want to be with me, and daddy hates me."

" And, so what! Mercedes this is your life, live it to the fullest. I'm behind you 100%. We'll make it through and be just fine."

CHAPTER TWENTY-ONE

Lord keep her please.

Shyann had just gotten a phone call from Henry saying that Megan was in the hospital. She got the girls and rushed to Kaiser. Henry was standing outside her room on his phone.

" I have to go." He whispered into the phone.

" Oh my gosh, Henry. What happened?" Shyann asked.

" I went to check on her and she was on the ground. I think she slipped and hit her head. She's unconscious!"

" Oh!" Shyann couldn't believe what he just said.

" Grandma!" Mercedes yelled and began crying.

" Calm down you guys." Henry screamed.

" Calm down, your telling me, my mom is not conscious and to calm down? Nigga please. Where is the fucking doctor?" Shyann hadn't cried in years and it was well needed. She fell to the ground and Mercedes held her. Henry didn't seem as upset for some reason.

" She'll be okay Shy." Henry said.

" Says who? I want to see the damn Doctor now!" She yelled.

" Their in there with her, wait til they come out."

" Mommy is grandma going to be okay?" Lexus cried.

" I don't know baby, I pray so."

They waited in the waiting room for an hour and the Doctor finally came out. Shyann eyes grew big and she stood up.

" Hi, I'm Dr.Helems." She extended her arm.

Shyann extended hers as well and they shook. "I'm Shyann Thomas, her daughter. How is she?"

" I'm very sorry, she's still unconscious. Look, it's not looking good, she hit her head and her brain is slowly bleeding. I'm sorry to say but. . ."

" Shyann cut her off, No! No! No!" She began screaming and crying. "God help me please." Shyann began to pray for she knew the power of prayer is the only thing that was able to save her mother.

" I'm sorry. I have to go back and check on her. Were just cleaning up and in a few minutes you guys can see her"

" Mama. I want grandma." Lexus cried.

" Me too."

Mercedes walked over to her mother and Lexus and gave her a hug. Henry just sat there with his hands covering his face. Shyann looked at Henry and his actions seemed weird. She told the girls to sit down and she walked over to him. She placed her hand on his shoulder and sat next to him.

" Are you okay?" Shyann asked.

" I'm fine." He began crying. "I just keep having flashback of Mama lying there. I didn't know what to think or do."

" It's okay Henry, you did the right thing."

" No, I should've called as soon as I got there."

" Well when did you call?"

" A few hours later."

" What? Why?" Shyann asked.

" I didn't know what to do. I was high."

" Nigga please." Shyann got in his face. "Nigga cush don't do that shit to you. High off what, you on some other shit."

" Man, I don't have to take this."

" You don't, you're the reason why Mama is going to die. You waited, they probably could've saved her." Shyann began crying and punching Henry in the chest.

" Man, move!" Henry pushed her. JJ came running down the hallway.

" Stop!" Every one in the waiting room was staring at them. Mercedes held Lexus as they cried. The Doctor and Security approached them.

" I'm going to have to ask you guys to leave." The Security officer said.

" No. Let them stay, I'll leave!" Henry said and walked down the hallway.

" Yeah, leave. Go get high or something!" Shyann screamed down the hallway.

" Mam, you're going to have to keep it down." The Security guy said.

" We good! We got you big homie." JJ replied as he guided Shyann to the chair to have a seat.

Shyann went in to see her Mama, she told the girls she'll call them in a few minutes. She wanted to be alone with her mother. Shyann eyes immediately began to feel with water. Megan lay there peacefully without a worry in the world. She had a slight smile and she looked happy. Shyann touched her hand and felt no life. Megan was dead and Shyann felt it.
" Mama." Shyann cried. "I love you so much." Shyann kissed her Mama on the hand and a tear fell from her cheek onto Megan's hand. All emotion had left Shyann's body as she lay next to her Mother.

Shyann hadn't talked to or seen Henry for 2days. She called everyone he knew and no one has seen him. JJ stayed with her and the girls at Shyann's house and catered to their every need. Shyann and the girls were asleep in the Den. Shyann left her phone on the table and it rang. JJ picked it up to see if he should awake Shyann or not, it was a text from Henry.
" Hey, Shy! We have to contact the Life Insurance Company."
JJ thought to himself why would that be his concern at the moment. He woke Shyann up and handed her the phone.
" This nigga crazy." Shyann said yarning.
" Exactly. Did the doctor's say how Megan slipped?"
" You know what! They didn't and I didn't even bother to ask. You thinking what I'm thinking."
" It's fucked up, but yeah ma."
Shyann and JJ drove to Megan's house to take a look around. They went into the kitchen to see if something was spilled on the floor or if whatever Megan tripped over was still on the ground. They didn't find anything. Shyann began to search the house and JJ went through the mail that was on the kitchen table. Shyann picked up the house phone and pressed redial.

" Quality Life Insurance, this is Jalissa. How may I help you?" Shyann just held the phone. "Hello." The lady repeated.
" I dialed the wrong number, sorry."

" Shy, come here!" JJ called.
" I pressed redial on the phone and it call Quality life insurance. I think that's kind of weird."
" I'm went threw the mail, did you know your mother had a policy for half a mill?"
" Let me see." She took the letter from JJ. "I knew she had insurance but I didn't know it was that much."
" Wait, look right there." JJ pointed to a name on the paper. "Henry Thomas."
" Mama had it in Mercedes name, I went with her like a few months ago to make the last payment and it was in Mercedes name."
" I may be wrong, but I feel I'm right. Shy, I don't think Megan fell and hit her head, I think someone hit her in the head." Shyann eyes began to fill with tears.
" Who would do something like that?"
" Whoever needed half a mill and knew it was only one way to get it."
" Naw, Henry wouldn't do anything like that."
" If Henry didn't do it personally, he hired someone to do it."
" Why though? If he needed money all he had to do was ask."
" He has been asking for money lately."
" That's true. Fuck, I'm going to kill his ass!"
" Wait, wait. We have to be sure first. This is serious."
" Fuck Henry! My fucking mother is laying in a hospital bed on life support and this nigga think he's about to get away with what he's done. Hell no!" Shyann began screaming and crying out.

Back at Shyann's place.
" Hey ma, how you feeling?" JJ asked Shyann as she lay on the bed crying.
" I don't know", tears began to roll down her face.

" I just got off the phone with one of my boys and they ran me up on game about Henry. They said he owe these Jamaicans like 200,000$! They said he was suppose to do a drop for them niggas and never showed. Word around Jamaica is that he hopped on a flight and shook with their money. Now some of them niggas flew out here to get their cash and kill him. They said Henry has until Friday to pay or they're going to kill him."

" So Henry killed Mama to get the Life Insurance money?"

" Looks like it!"

" Fuck, what's today?"

" Monday."

" We got into it at the hospital, he told me he waited a few hours then took my mother to the hospital. The last call was to the Insurance Company, it should've been to 911."

" Yeah, but he probably used his cell."

" True." Shyann sat up and got dressed.

" Where you going ma?"

CHAPTER TWENTY-TWO

Bull shit!

Shyann drove to Quality Insurance. She left the girls home and told them to stay in the house until she got back. JJ accompanied her and start making phone to see if anyone had a location on Henry.

Shyann and JJ sat down to talk to Sherry; the woman that had been dealing with Megan's policy since she opened it.

" Well see. . .", she pointed on the computer screen. "It says online change from Mercedes Blake to Henry Thomas, and dispute Lexus Blake."

" Okay so she had them as first and secondary and Henry took them off." Shyann whispered.

" Excuse me."

" Ummm, nothing. You know, my mother and I come in here all the time! Has anyone else come with her?"

" The last time I saw the two of you, you made the last payment."

" Right."

" A gentlemen came in a few days ago, he was tall and dark."

" Henry."

" Yes, I remember he showed me his ID and said he was her son. He asked me if I could look up her policy, he had all her information and said she was sick. He asked how long would it take the family member to get paid after death? I thought it was weird but his name was on the policy so I gave him the information. I asked was something wrong with Megan and he just said she was sick and the family was worried about not having money to bury her."

" My mother is on Life Support at the moment and I'm praying she pulls through."

" I am so sorry to hear that, Shyann we never received the return policy on the change."

" What do you mean?"

" When we have online changes done, we have mandatory confirmation letters sent out. The change cannot be made unless you return the letter and we approve it. We try to protect our customers from fraudualit activity occurring without them knowing."

" Is this the letter right here?" Shyann reached in her purse and pulled out the letter JJ found in the kitchen.

" Yes it is." Shyann tore the letter in half and then tore it in half again.

" That nigga is dumb wild." JJ turned to Shyann and said.

" He's on some hard ass drugs that got him in some deep shit."

" Man, he better be praying because God is the only one that can save him once we catch his ass." JJ said rubbing his hands together.

Shyann and JJ went to the hospital to check on Megan. She doctor smiled as she saw them.

" I take it you have good news?" JJ said.

" What's up?" Shyann asked.

" Okay the bleeding stopped. I don't know how or why, were running some tests now she's still on Life Support though. We maybe able to do surgery now, bad news is, she maybe brain damaged."

" Well, she's a fighter and always has been. I'll take care of her, please just get my mother home and out of here."

" We're trying our hardest."

" Thank you Jesus!" Shyann said, as Doctor smiled and walked away. JJ put his arm around Shyann and hugged her.

" She's going to be okay."

" I thought she was dead when I lay beside her." Shyann began to cry on his chest.

Tuesday!

Shyann called Henry and pretended like everything was cool and acted as if she wasn't onto him. He agreed to come by the house at noon to talk about Mama. Shyann hadn't told him that Megan had chances of survival. Henry assumed she was already dead. Mercedes dropped Lexus off at School and went to Nate's mother house talk and have lunch. JJ looked at Henry like a brother and hated his guts for doing what he did to Megan.

Henry pulled into the driveway and got out. She opened the door before he had enough time to press the doorbell.

" Damn! I can't knock." He looked high and had the same clothes on from the hospital.

" Henry, you smell bad."

" I know, I'm stressing." They walked over and sat at the kitchen table. Shyann couldn't take the smell so she opened the kitchen window. She noticed a white Benz sitting outside with two black dudes sitting in the car. She didn't trip she just made a mental note and sat back down.

" So what's up, I haven't heard from you since Friday at the hospital. The police came asking all these questions. I don't know what happened, I told them to talk to you." She said lying, trying to get him to talk.

" I went to check on Mama and she saw me and I guess I scared her and she turned and slipped on some cooking oil."

Shyann remembered him saying he found her lying on the ground, now he saying he saw her fall.

" Oh, so you saw her fall."

" Yeah, it was like a dream. I couldn't move."

" That's why you waited to take her to the hospital?"

" Yeah." Henry looked like a ghost. He couldn't stay focus, his eyes had no life they were baggy and red.

" Henry, what are you on?"

" Man."

" I'm not dumb, we grew up around addicts all our lives and I know one when I see one."

" Man, get off me. I'm about to go."

" Naw, little big brother. What's up with the life insurance money?"

" I don't know we need to pay for Mama's funeral."

Shyann began laughing. "Mama funeral?"

" Yeah, what's funny?"

" Junkie." She laughed again. "Mama ain't dead!"

" What?" Henry jumped up.

" She ain't dead. Damn, you seem disappointed."

" She was dead when I took her to the hospital."

" Naw little big brother, she was unconscious." Shyann replied being a smart ass. "Maybe you should visit her. Oh, yeah and you can't receive money from an Insurance company without an death certificate dumb ass."

" What are you talking about?"

" Henry you remember who you're fucking with. I'm smarter than your dumb ass. You tried to kill Mama, talking about she slipped and then you found her on the floor. You fucking weak ass junkie, you hit Mama in the head with something and when I find out, I'm going to kill you myself."

" Shyann what the fuck are you talking about. I didn't kill Mama, I wouldn't do anything like that. I swear to God."

" I said my Mama ain't dead! You keep talking like she dead nigga. You owe them niggas bread and you need it by Friday. You thought you could kill Mama, get the money and pay them off. You tried to kill my Mama nigga! Get the fuck out my house and my life, nigga we ain't ken. Fuck you!"

" Shyann I didn't try to kill her. You have to believe me. How do you know I owe people money? Look, I need your help."

" Nigga are you hard at hearing? I said get the fuck out! You want me to call the police and you explain the story to them? You thought you could get away with this shit homie? Fuck out my face."

" Shy, help me I need 100,000$ more to get them off my back."

" Fuck you!" Shyann spit in his face and pushed him out the back door.

" Fuck!" He screamed.

Henry walked along the side of the house to his car as Shyann watched from the window. Shyann saw the white Benz follow Henry.

" Damn! This bitch ass nigga had them follow him to my house." She said aloud to herself. "Fuck!" She socked the wall, leaving a fist size whole.

She smashed over to JJ's to tell him what happened. She walked up the stairs and heard a woman's voice.

" Please, not today." She said to herself. She knocked on the door and JJ answered.

" What's up ma?" Shyann walked in and saw a girl sitting on the sofa.

" What's up? Who is this JJ?"

" Chill ma, this Henry ex." JJ kissed Shyann and smiled. "I've never seen you jealous, it's sexy." Shyann smiled.

" Shut up. I thought I was about to have to kill this hoe."

" Hey, I'm Robin."

" What's up? I'm Shy, Henry's sister. How long were yall together?" She asked talking a seat next to her.

" We broke up 5 months ago. We were together for 10 months."

" Oh, okay. Do you know what kind of drugs my brother are on?"

" Lean, sniff dope and pops pills anything he could get his hands on really. That's why were not together anymore, I couldn't handle his lifestyle."

" Let me guess, he's the father?" Shyann asked looking at her round belly.

" Yeah, when we broke up I was 3months and I didn't tell him because I was going to get an abortion."

" What made you decide to keep it?"

" I think it was a sign from God, I went to my appointment and the doctor told me my fever was too high and she didn't want me to take the risk. I just took it as a sign from God to keep him and here we are." She smiled and rubbed her belly.

" Yeah. How long has my brother been hooked?"

" I say for about a year. At first I didn't know then he left some stuff in the bathroom and I asked him about it. I didn't want to leave him like that so I stuck around. It got bad though, he began stealing from me, and hitting me. I finally got enough courage to say, enough and I left." Robin bowed her head.

" Damn, sorry to hear that."

" I've been trying to find him and tell him about the baby. He has a right to know and I do want him apart of his life if he chooses to be."

" I see." Shyann began to tell JJ what happened when Henry came by.

CHAPTER TWENTY-THREE

Off the wall!

Henry goes to the hospital to talk to the doctor about Megan. He was acting weird and the doctor could sense something was wrong.

" Is everything okay?" She said smiling.

" Oh, yeah. I'm just concerned about my mother that's all."

" Well she's doing great and the surgery went well."

" Surgery?"

" Yes sir, she made it through, we got the blood clod. Would you like to see her? She's still in a coma but she fighting hard and should pull through shortly." Henry stood there with a disappointed look on his face. "Are you okay?"

" Just shocked."

" Well smile, your mother is going to be okay."

" May I see her?"

" Sure. Take all the time you need."

Henry walked over to Megan and began to cry. "What have I done?" He said to himself. Henry looked at the machine Megan was hooked up too and eye balled the plugs. He reached over to unplug the machine out of the wall and the doctor walked in and he jumped.

" What are you doing?"

" I. . .ummmm. . ." Henry couldn't think of anything to say. "My pen fell", he smiled.

" Okay, I'm going to ask you to stand on this side please."

" Oh, okay no problem. I was just leaving anyways." Megan moved her right hand.

" Oh, did you see that?" The doctor asked staring at Megan's hand.

" No. What happened?"

" She just moved her hand."

" Oh, what does that mean?"

" She's fighting. Look she just did it again."

" Oh." Henry said in a dry tone. "I have to go pick up my daughter from School." Henry said lying. "I'm going to come right back."

" Okay, tell your family your mother is doing well."

" I will." Henry left and the white Benz followed him.

Letting go.

Chris wouldn't give up on Mercedes he called her everyday. He had got tired of Mercedes ignoring him. He sat outside her house until she pulled up. He knew everyday she picked up Mercedes and assumed they were going straight home. Mercedes and Lexus finally pulled up and Chris yelled through the window.

" Mercedes!" She turned to look and grabbed Lexus and walked faster. He got out the car and ran towards them.

" Mercedes, I need to talk." Chris begged.

" Lexus go in the house, ill be in, in a few minutes."

" Okay." Lexus replied.

" What Chris?"

" I thought you were getting an abortion."

" Yeah, I tried but I couldn't go through with it."

" Why didn't you tell me?"

" Tell you for what Chris?"

" Look, you don't have to like me. I'm the baby's father and I deserve to know what's going on."

" What's going on is, you and Porsha and how you'd disrespect me like that."

" I'm sorry."

" Me too, you had something good and you choose to mess it up. Chris I don't trust you and we will never be together again! Ever!"

" You don't mean that."

" I don't? Okay, actions speak louder than words. I'll show you I mean it."

" After all we been through. . ."

Mercedes cut him off. "No after all you put me through, I'm done. I ain't ask for none of this shit, but that's the cards I pulled."

" What does that mean?"

" Chris, bye! That's what it means."

" What about the baby?"

" My baby is going to be just fine, were moving to Atlanta."

" When were you going to tell me?"

Mercedes laughed. "I'm telling you now." Mercedes walked in the house a closed the door. She stood there and watched him walk to the car and she began to cry.

Mercedes loved Chris but felt it was best for them to be apart. He hurt her and dogged her out, something she thought he'd never do to her. She felt like when she needed him the most he wasn't there, now he wants to pretend like he wants the baby. She just wanted him to go to College and live his life.

Chris wanted to be with Mercedes and knew he messed up. He told himself he would do anything and everything to get her back. That evening Chris went home and went online to Georgia State and Morehouse. His ultimate dream was to go to USC but with the baby on the way he decided to put that dream on hold. Chris was starting quarterback and knew he could get a scholarship to any School in the US.

CHAPTER TWENTY-FOUR

Let's play!

Shyann sat outside Meeka's house while smoking a blunt. She knew she had work that night and would be pulling up anytime after 2am. Shyann was stressed out and didn't care about anything at the moment. She placed her 9 in her lap and patiently wanted. She didn't know what to do everything was going wrong in her life and she was no longer in control. When she saw Meeka's green Ford Focus She quietly got out of the car and approached her.

When Meeka saw Shyann standing next to the drivers door she tried to lock it, but Shyann was too quick and already opened the door. Shyann took the 9 and beat Meeka in the face. Meeka put her hands over her face to block from getting hit, but Shyann was swinging too fast for her. Meeka managed to kick Shyann in the stomach causing her to fall back. Shyann saw Meeka reach in the back under the passengers seat and Shyann popped her. She assumed she was reaching for her heat and Shyann didn't wait to find out. She quickly became deaf from the fire.

Meeka was still breathing, the bullet hit her in the chest. Shyann gave her one to the head and jogged to her truck and left. Shyann head was all fucked up at this point and she began to act without thinking. She went home to take a shower, she checked on the girls and headed back into the streets.

She drove up and down the streets of L.A. searching for her brother. Shyann couldn't stop thinking about Megan and how Henry could do something like this. She had so much built up anger she felt she needed to release. Shyann drove for 45 minutes and Henry was nowhere to be found. She saw the same white Benz that was outside her house parked on 1st and Cope. Shyann parked a few cars behind the car and waited.

She jumped up and realized she'd dozed off, the clock read 5:30am. She wanted to get out of there before sunrise so no one would see her. She stared to start the car and saw the same two dudes walking to the car. She ducked her head and watched them pull off, then followed behind them. She wrote down the licenses plate number and kept her distance. She heard her cell phone ring and reached in her purse to answer it.

" Hello."

" Mama, come quick. It's Henry." Mercedes yelled through the phone.

" Okay, calm down what happened?"

" I don't know he's bleeding really bad."

" Okay, I'm on the way." Shyann stopped following the car and drove to her house. She pulled into the driveway and rushed inside the house.

" What happened?" Shyann asked Henry. He had two black eyes and his nose was broken. He covered his side with his hand, Shyann lifted up his hand and he had been cut really deep. "Oh my gosh, Henry what happened?"

" These nigga want their money, they paid me a reminder visit."

" Go get some towels Cedes, I need to stop the bleeding."

" Tomorrow Friday, I need 100,000 more dollars."

" Fuck Henry! Today is Friday its 6am." Shyann yelled, Merceded handed her mom the towels. "I'll give you the fucking cash to get these niggas off your back. I fucking hate your guts but how I feel right now, if anybody is going to murder you it's going to be me."

Henry looked at Shyann and didn't really pay attention to nothing she said. All he heard was that, she'll give him the money.

" You need to go to the hospital."

" I'll go later, I have to pay them niggas at 10."

" AM?"

" PM!"

" You're dumb as fuck, you didn't notice them niggas following you?"

" Naw, they were?"

" You mean are, it's a white Benz outside now. I noticed they were following you when you came by the other day. Man Henry how could you be so dumb?"

" Man I don't know, I know I fucked up."

" You really did. Robin is pregnant."

" What?"

" JJ caught up with her for me and we chopped it up for a minute. You're in some deep shit my nigga and it's fucked up."

Shyann cleaned Henry up and wrapped his side to stop the blood. Shyann told Mercedes to walk with him to the Den and lay him down. Shyann went to her bedroom and grabbed her 38 and tucked it in the back of her jeans and grabbed a nice size potato from the kitchen.
" I'm about to go outside for a second. I'll be right back."
" Okay." Mercedes replied.
Shyann walked up to the Benz and tapped on the window, the driver rolled down the window. Shyann placed the potato inside her hoody pocket.
" Yeah!" The driver answered, his skin was really dark and he had a scar across his forehead. He spoke with an ascent and his mouth was filled with gold teeth.
" Listen here, I'm going to say this one time and one time only! You and your bitch ass boss lay another hand on my fucking brother, I will personally kill yall myself. If yall want yall fucking money tonight I suggest you get the fuck out of here right now."
" Bitch please!"
Shyann gave a slight laugh. "See you just had to piss me off. If anybodies a bitch it's yall pussy ass niggas, running around taking orders from another man."
" Bitch, get out of here and go back to your family tramp", he said continuing looking forward towards the street. Shyann couldn't take the disrespect anymore, she quickly reached behind her back and released the safety and cocked her heat back. She pulled out the potato and placed it in front of the 38 gave that nigga one to the head. The guy on the passenger side reached under his seat and Shyann gave that nigga one to the head as well. She used the potato so the fire shots wouldn't be loud and draw attention.
" Fuck!" She said to herself. She knew by doing that the situation was going to turn out worse than it was intentionally. She ran across the street and told Henry and Cedes to go to JJ's house. Lexus was still asleep she woke her up and carried her to her truck. It was a little after

7am when they arrived at JJ's. Shyann had a key so she just let herself in and told everyone to chill in the living room.

" JJ." Shyann whispered in his ear for him to awake.

" What's up?" He opened his eyes. "Ma you got blood all on you."

" I know, I had to blast these niggas real quick."

" What?" JJ sat up. "What the fuck happened Ma?"

" Man, first I blasted that bitch Meeka."

JJ cut her off. "Ma you doing too much."

" I know, man them niggas beat up Henry and stabbed him, so I blasted them too."

" Ma, you doing too much. You need to slow the fuck down, like real shit. You think you're just so fucking untouchable. Reality check for that ass, you're NOT!"

" Damn, nice to know how you feel about me." Shyann got up and walked towards the door.

" Wait you know I didn't mean it like that." JJ stood up wearing nothing but his boxers.

" Yeah, well Henry and the kids are in the living room."

" What? You brought that bitch ass nigga to my crib."

" JJ come on, that's my brother."

" Yeah, you keep in mind the same brother that tried to kill your Mama."

" I know." She put her head down. "I'm going to handle it as soon as shit settle down. That's my word! But I'm going to give this nigga that 100 g's."

" This nigga tried to kill Megan and you're about to help bail this nigga out. Get the fuck out of here, are you serious. Man fuck that nigga!"

" JJ that's my brother and it would kill my Mama to find out JJ dead."

" He didn't think it'll kill you to find out she was dead, did he?"

" I feel where you coming from, but trust me. I know exactly what I'm doing." Shyann didn't have a clue to what she was doing and wasn't aware of the danger she was putting herself into either. Shyann always kept a spare of clean clothes in her car for her and the girls just incase they had to up and leave on day. She sent Mercedes down to get her black Gucci duffle bag. They all showered and got dressed. JJ didn't say a word to Henry, Henry spoke and JJ walked pass as if he didn't exist because in his eyes he was already dead to him.

CHAPTER TWENTY-FIVE

God is good!

Shyann and the girls went to visit Megan at the hospital. Megan was doing very well and was responding. When Megan saw her mother feeding herself she began to cry tears of joy. She felt as if weights lifted off her shoulders and she was relieved.

" Mama." Shyann cried.

" Hey baby." Megan spoke slow and soft, as a smile appeared on her face.

" God is so good."

" Hey babies", she said to Mercedes and Lexus.

" Hi grandma", Lexus ran to hug her. "I missed you."

" I missed you too grandma." Mercedes said.

" Give me a hug, how's the baby doing?"

" Were doing fine, better now that we know your okay."

" You're getting big." Mercedes just smiled. "Where is Henry?"

" Hey Cedes, take Lexus down to the Cafeteria and get her some breakfast." She handed her a 20$ bill.

" Okay, you want something Mama?"

" Ummm, some orange juice."

" Okay."

Shyann pulled a chair close to Megan's bed. "Mama do you remember what happened the day you fell?"

" Child, I don't. Where is Henry?"

" Mama, I need you to try and remember."

" Baby, you're scaring me is Henry okay?"

" He's fine Mama, he's at JJ's house."

" Well why didn't he come see me?" Shyann wanted to tell her what was going on but knew she'd been through enough already.

" He has the flu and didn't want to pass it to you. He has a baby on the way."

" When did this happen?"

" I don't know, I don't even know the girl. Her name Robin."

" Oh, I remember him mentioning that name before."

"Mama, your memory is there you just have to try harder to pull everything back together. I really need to know what happened the day you fell, can you try for me please?"

Megan closed her eyes. "I'm trying, it's just so hard."

"Okay Mama, its okay. You'll come around sooner than later." Shyann and Megan continued to talk and exercise her memory.

JJ didn't trust that nigga Henry so he made him sit outside while he was downstairs serving and shit. Every time JJ looked up at Henry he wanted that nigga dead more and more.

"JJ, I'm about to hit a few corners I'll be right back."

"Naw nigga, you staying put homie."

"I need to handle some business." Henry attempted to walk pass JJ ignoring what he had said.

"Man homie chill, shit back down. You're weak as fuck and I'm not letting you out of my eye site until Shy come back."

"I need to go get that 100g's from the spot."

"Don't trip I'll take you."

"Naw, I have to go alone. You don't know them people on that side of town."

"Look homie, I ain't no bitch! You seem like you on some bull shit homie and if it wasn't for your sister your ass would've been dead homie."

"Nigga fuck you, you're the one that's about to be dead. Nate got his peoples keeping tabs on your ass." JJ punched that nigga in the jaw and Henry flew to the ground.

"Fuck you and fuck Nate homie. Your bitch ass trying to leave to got get high, here nigga." JJ threw him a little bag with coke. "Bitch ass."

The doctor's said Megan would be discharged on Monday they just wanted to fun a few more tests. Shyann was excited for he mom and knew she'd pull through. She told Mercedes to follow her to the house and pack some clothes so they could stay at their cousin house for the weekend. When she pulled up to the house it was about 3pm and officers had the streets blocked off.

" Fuck!" She said to herself. She parked down the block as well as Mercedes and they walked to the house.

" You can't come down this street mam." The officer said.

" I live here." Shyann reached in her purse and showed the officer her ID. "My baby is sick and I need to get her medicine out the house please."

" Okay, come through."

" Stay close." She said to the girls.

" Mama what happened?" Lexus asked.

" Looks like someone got shot baby? Hurry up."

When they got in the house she told the girls to quickly pack some clothes and put them in your backpacks.

" Mama I don't want to use my backpack my books are in them." Lexus said.

Shyann took her backpack and tipped it over causing everything to fall out. "Now there are no books, do what I said!" Lexus head fell and she packed her clothes.

" You don't have to be snappy with her."

" Mercedes shut the hell up, I'm tired of your smart ass mouth." Mercedes closed her room door.

" Let's be out in 5 minutes please." Shyann yelled down the hallway.

Shyann shut her bedroom blinds and pulled the curtains closed, and locked the door. She went into her walk in closet and removed her body mirror she had placed on the wall. It was a door that led to a tiny room upstairs. Shyann had a close friend that's a contractor build it in before she moved into the house.

Shyann had a million dollars cash in 100$ bills up there. She had 10 black duffle bags all filled with 100,000$ each. She grabbed one and went back down the stairs. Her shirt had gotten dirty and had a few cob weds on it, so she took it off. She placed the mirror back like she had it and grabbed two pairs of jeans and closed the closet door.

She reached inside her drawers to put on a white shit that read "Bad Ass" then continued packing the rest of her clothes. She put her clothes in a large tote bag and went to get the girls. "Yall ready?" She yelled.

" Coming." Mercedes said.

Shyann kissed the girls bye and told them she'll see them Monday. Mercedes and Lexus drove to their cousin, Zayla's house in Orange County. Lexus hugged Shyann really tight.

" Sorry I didn't listen earlier Mama."

" Oh, Lexus it's okay, sorry I snapped at you. Mommy is just going through a lot right now. I love you very much and I want you to listen to Zay and your sister.

" Look Ma, I'm a little wiser than Lexus. Be careful I know something is going down." Mercedes gave her a hug. "I love you always."

" Baby, I love you too. You two stop it I'll see my best girls on Monday, right?" Shyann smiled and they both shook their heads yes. "Here!" Shyann handed Mecedes 500$. "Take care off all needs first and keep a close eye on your sister."

Shyann drove back to JJ's apartment. JJ was standing outside talking to some of his little homies. When they saw Shyann walk up the spoke and went back to work.

" Hey baby." Shyann said then kissed him on the lips.

" What's up Ma?" He pulled her closer and hugged her.

" Where Henry?"

" That nigga sleep on the coach. That nigga needs to get to the hospital and get his side checked out."

" I know, I told him. He said he's going to go later tonight after the drop. I wanna go with him."

" The hell you ain't!"

" Man that's my brother!"

"It's too dangerous and you don't know how to act. You got two kids to look after, if something happens to you. . ."

"Okay!" Shyann cut him off. "He made this bed now he has to lay in it."

"That nigga ain't shit anyways, I know that's your brother and all but that nigga tried to kill Megan! I know he did."

Henry waited on Warehouse road dressed in all black. He was very weak and was still loosing blood. He kept looking at his guess watch and checking his cell phone to see if he had a missed call. It was midnight and he stood alone in the dark alley with the wind blowing. Henry saw a Black Escalade pull up with the lights off.

"Drop the duffle bag and take 10 steps backwards." A deep voice yelled through the window.

"Okay." Henry dropped the bag and took 10 steps back like he was instructed to do. He lifted his hands to the sky and felt a sharp pain run across his side. Without thinking he grabbed his side to ease the pain and gun shots fired from the truck. They thought he was reaching for his heat and they took him out before, he had a chance to take them out.

Henry was bare and wasn't strapped he flew to the ground. The passenger got out of the truck and approached him pointing his gun to his head.

"Is he dead?" The driver yelled.

"Yup!" He grabbed the duffle bag and got into the truck and they sped off into the dark. Henry lay there helplessly and blood was everywhere.

Megan woke up out of her sleep trying to catch her breath. She had been sweating really bad and she had a fever. Megan knew in her heart that something was wrong she could feel it. She immediately began to pray and seek God. Tears began to fall from her eyes and she had a feeling of someone cutting her stomach open.

Shyann sat at the red light waiting for it to change green. She was about two blocks from her house on this late foggy night. She drove in silence with both her windows rolled completely down. The streets were empty as she thought about running the red light. A dark blue Impala pulled up beside her, she glanced over to look and the back window rolled down. Bullets began to strike Shyann's car. She quickly ducked and put her car in reverse, leaving tire marks on the ground.

Shyann reached for her 38 from under the seat and fired back. She made a quick left on the first side street she saw. The Impala sped off into the fog. Shyann kept looking into her rear view mirror to see if they followed her. "Fuck!" She said aloud to herself. She couldn't believe what just happened. The same people that killed Henry were after her. She killed two of their boys and they wanted her dead.

Shyann didn't know what to do at the moment. She had never got caught off guard like that. Her truck had 5 bullet holes and the back window had gotten shot out so glass was everywhere. She drove to Enterprise by the LAX Airport, she knew they were 24 hours and needed a ride. She called her mechanic and told him she's parking her car there and could he pick it up in the morning and fix it.

Shyann rented a small SUV, it wasn't anything luxury like she wanted, but it would do. It was a White Toyota Pilot. She thought about if she should call JJ and tell him what happened. She decided to wait until she saw him. She merged on the 405S and headed towards his house. When she pulled up Mercedes car was parking out front. She parked behind her car and rolled a blunt. She didn't want to smoke in the house with the girls, she texted JJ to come downstairs.
When he walked downstairs he didn't see her car so he began to head back upstairs to get out the cold. Shyann gently pressed the horn and JJ walked towards the truck.

" Where your car at?" JJ asked as he walked up to the truck.
" Get in."

" What's up ma?" He hugged and kissed her on the lips. "Where your car at?"

" You heard from Henry?" Shyann asked passing him the cush blunt she just rolled. "You wanna hit this?" JJ took the blunt from her and pressed it against his lips and inhaled the smoke.

" I ain't heard from that nigga, you? And why do I have to keep asking who truck this is?"

" No, and it's a rental. My shit got shot up." JJ faced dropped and heart began to beat fast.

" What?" He shouted. "Man by who? I'm about to get my heat." JJ reached to open the door and Shyann pulled his arm.

" Damn, JJ wait. I'm not sure who did it. I think it was them nigga's Henry owe but I'm not sure."

" Did you see their faces?" JJ closed the door and took his seat.

" Naw! But I know it was them."

" Man, you know you been moving fast lately. It could be anybody, I be telling your ass to shit down somewhere."

" I know, I know. Do you think I want to hear that shit JJ?"

" Don't come at me like that ma, I'm not the enemy shit."

" I know, my fault." She kissed him on the lips and he held her tight.

Chapter Twenty-Six

Thanksgiving.

The holiday approached fast. Things began to quiet down and Shyann hasn't ran into any trouble in the past few weeks. She began to feel like she was getting her life back together. Megan was doing well and her memory was slowly coming back. God is good and Megan prays and seek God every day. Chris and Mercedes were doing well and he spent the day with her and the family.

Shyann cooked ham, turkey, greens, stuffing and gravy, mac & cheese, candied yams and corn bread. For desert she made sweet potato pie, a German chocolate cake that looked tasteful, and Megan's favorite banana pudding. The food looked delicious and they all sat at the table and prepared to enjoy the lovely day.

Henry was still missing and no one in the neighborhood had heard anything about it. Megan knew in her heart that her baby was dead but didn't want to believe it. They had signs everywhere and contacted the police 24 hors after they hadn't heard from him. JJ did everything he could do to find out what went down. People in L.A. run their mouths and it wouldn't be long until someone started talking.

Every year Megan usually does all the cooking and everyone goes to her house. Since the accident Shyann wanted her mother close so she's been staying with her and the girls. Shyann loved her mother and would do anything for her. How she fell was still blurry to her and she tries everyday to help Megan try to remember. Shyann had faith in her mom and knew she'll come through soon.

" May I say grace?" Mercedes asked.
" Yes, actually, you can start but I want everyone to go around and say something."

" Okay, everyone hold hands and bow your head. God we thank you for bringing us all together and blessing us with life and this wonderful meal. God protect our daily journey and keep us covered with you blood and loving protection. Thank you Lord for bringing my granny home to us safely. Bless me and my baby, and Lord please bless Chris and I to raise this child in your will." Mercedes opened her eyes and smiled at Chris. She gave a little pull to his hand and he picked up the prayer.

He cleared his throat. "God it's Chris Malton, I know I don't talk to you much, but I am very thankful. Thank you for my family and thanks for this family for taking me in. Lord I'm not perfect, but if you show me the way, I'll follow and try my hardest. God please let me be a good dad and be there for my baby. Lord forgive me for hurting Mercedes and bless us with another chance. Thank you, oh yeah, and bless Shyann for making this good looking food." Giggles ran across the table, as Lexus picked up the prayer.

" God we are very thankful for this day and for our lives. God please bless my daddy right now, and Lord please find my Uncle Henry and tell him to come home. Tell him we miss him and we love him. God thank you for my granny and my mommy. Thank you for letting me be a auntie to my sister baby and for getting good grades in School. Thank you for JJ in our lives and for him always being there for me. Amen."

" Don't close it out yet Lexus." Shyann whispered. "Father God in the mane of Jesus, forgive me of all my sins Lord Jesus. God I want to thank you for life and keeping my family safe. God we may not be the perfect family but you know our hearts Lord and you're able to chance our ways. God I look around and I'm blessed, thank you for this meal and being surrounded by people who love me." Shyann paused and JJ picked up the prayer.

" Ummm, God I'm not really used to doing this but I'll give it my all. You always got my back and look out for me. Thank you for blessing me with these wonderful people in my life and Shyann is my better half. I love her, thanks for allowing me to love. Thank you for Megan, she's such a strong solider and pulling through. The doctors said she wasn't gonna make it and look at her, she's here." Tears began to roll down their faces.

"They say with you all things are possible and without nothing is possible. That's so true, look at this family despite all they been through, their blessed and I'm grateful to be apart of this family." JJ said.

Megan began to speak. "Lord we love you. Love we love you." She spoke in a very low tone as tears rolled down her face. "God you've been more than good to this family and we love you. Keep everyone at this table covered with your blood, for it's a dangerous walk out there. Bless these kids Lord and show them the way, teach them to walk in faith. Lord you said, no weapon formed against us shall prosper and I believe it in my heart Lord Jesus.
Lord pick up my son, wherever he is right now and breath new life into him and allow him to follow you Lord. Forgive him Lord, he didn't mean to…" Megan paused and let out a scream. She had a flashback and saw Henry push her down from behind. "Lord have your will be done. Thank you for this meal and this family. In Jesus name Amen. Excuse me for a minute."

Megan went to the restroom to wash her face and cried into the washcloth. Shyann came in behind her and didn't ask what was wrong, she knew. She embraced her mother with a hug and they both shared tears on each other's shoulders.

Megan remembered that day like it was yesterday. She was boiling some hot water and Henry tapped at the back door. She went over to unlock it and turned to walk back towards the kitchen. Henry knew he couldn't hurt his mother looking her in the eyes so he pushed her. Megan fell face down and hit her head on the corner of the counter top next to the stove. Henry was high and his focus was off.

He searched through the house looking for cash and couldn't believe what he had done. He sat next to his mother for an hour crying and regretting what happened and finally decided to call 911. He told the police she slipped and fell and hit her head. He thought she was dead on sight, to only find out later that she wasn't. Henry did all that for some damn insurance money that he wouldn't have gotten anyways.

Sometimes you have to stop and ask yourself, "What matters most?" Because reality of life and situations we all face daily, doesn't matter at all. When you die and leave this place what can you really take with you? All the money and drugs in the world were designed to kill and destroy you. So what really matters, when nothing matters at all!

" Did Henry push you?" Shyann whispered.
" It's in Gods hands now child." Megan replied.

That was enough for Shyann to understand the answer to the question. She couldn't believe Henry would lie in her face. All this over some damn insurance money, she thought to herself. She wanted to find Henry alive so she could kill him herself. But little did she know for sure, he was already dead!

Chapter Twenty-Seven

5 months!

Mercedes was really excited to find out what she was having. Chris wanted a boy and Mercedes wanted a girl but whatever they had they would be happy. Mercedes belly was big and round, the doctor did the ultrasound and showed Mercedes the monitor. She pointed out two bodies and told Mercedes, "looks like twins."

Mercedes looked at Chris. "What?"

" Twins?" Chris relied.

" Yes, looks like two healthy girls", the doctor said.

" Wow, I don't know if I can handle two babies. One, I can do, but two? I don't know." Mercedes said.

" We'll be fine", Chris smiled and held her hand. "We'll make it together."

Shyann received a call from the police station saying they believe they may have found Henry's body and needed her to come down and identify it. She and Megan drove to the morgue and saw Henry's body. Megan immediately began breaking down and sobbing.

" My baby, what did they do to my baby?" Megan screamed.

For some reason Shyann couldn't spare a tear for her brother. She was very much angry and sad but she showed no emotions. She loved her brother with her heart and soul and couldn't understand why he would try to take their mother's life. Shyann was disappoint in her brother and the decisions he choose to make and she felt death was a good place for him right now.

Shyann held Megan close and comforted her as she stared at her brother's face. She asked herself, who was he? She looked at him like she was looking a ghost, a human with no soul or heart. Shyann hated her brother more and more as she stood there and wanted to spit in his face. Her kids only uncle was dead, her only brother was dead.

" God have mercy on my brother please." She whispered to herself.

Mercedes and Chris were at the house when Shyann pulled into the driveway. Mercedes began to prepare dinner, she looked through the window and saw her granny crying and dropped the empty frying pan and ran outside. She knew something wasn't right. Chris looked from the window, unsure if he should follow or not. He saw Shyann tell her something and Mercedes fell to her knees and began screaming.

Chris ran outside and held her. "What's wrong?" Chris asked.

" He's dead!" Mercedes screamed.

Chris never lost anyone close to him so he didn't know how she was feeling. All he could do was hold her tight and kiss her on the forehead.

Funeral!

About a week later Henry was buried. Shyann didn't attend the funeral, she sent the kids with JJ and Megan. It was too much for her and she couldn't stand to see her brother. The service was held at Holy Way, the same church Henry had been baptized at when he was 7 years old. Robin was there with their 4 weeks old baby boy. She named him Henry Jr. He was cute and cubby, didn't cry that much

The church was filled and people stood on the sidewalk awaiting to get in. Henry was loved indeed, took a few bad turns in life and getting hooked on cocaine but overall he was most envied and admired with his charm. The service was good and everyone in the room left out in tears.

Shyann watched CSI on the coach, while sipping on Ciroc and lemonade and smoking her brains out. "That fucker!" She said to herself and laughed aloud. "Fucker tried to kill my mama, any last words Henry." Shyann began to break down in tears and continued to sip her cup. The pain was too much for her to handle and didn't want to face the reality of Henry being dead and trying to kill Megan.

She went into her bathroom and ran a hot bubble bath. She was high off cush and was tipsy off her drink. She felt good and just wanted to relax. She took off her clothes and stood bare in front of the mirror. She pulled her long pretty hair into a bun and washed her face. The tub was almost full so she turned off the water and grabbed her ipod. She began listening to Keyshia Cole and Monica, trust.

Just as she was about to put her foot in she heard the doorbell ring. "Damnit!" She said aloud, she grabbed her robe and put it on. "Bitch can't never have peace, who the fuck is it?" She yelled walking towards the door, no one replied. She opened the door and no one was there.

" Why do motha fuckas feel like playing with me today?" As she was closing the door she saw a note tapped on the door. It read: *Simple minded bitches like you don't deserve to live and breath the same air as me.*

Shyann laughed aloud, closed the door and set the alarm. She placed the note on the counter and went back to her bubble bath. "Was that supposed to scare me or something? Ha!" She laughed again.

A few hours later Megan, the girls and JJ came home. Shyann was sleep in her bedroom. JJ saw the note on the counter and grabbed it to read. She went down the hallway to Shyann's room. He gave a little tap on the door the opened it slowly. He saw she was asleep so he sat on the bed and whispered in her ear.

" Ma, wake up." He gave her arm a little tug. "Ma! Wake up baby." Shyann eyes opened. "Hey baby."

" Hey." Shyann said rubbing her eyes. "What time is it?"

" It's like 7 something."

" Damn, how long I been sleep?"

" I don't know we just got here. You been drinking and shit, where this note come from?" JJ asked showing her the paper.

" Man somebody playing games and shit. I think it's funny." She began laughing. JJ saw the empty bottle of Ciroc by the bed.

" You drank that whole 5th today?"

" Sure did, and smoked a 8th!" She giggled. "I'm popping huh?" She laughed. JJ knew how she felt and knew she was doing all of this to cover up the pain.

" Did you eat?"

" I had a little bowl of cereal, I wasn't really hungry. I'm not drunk, I'm just chillin." She said with a straight face.

" I know, I know you, you okay?" JJ grabbed her hand and asked.

" I'll be just fine, what other choice do I have?"

" It's okay to show you're hurt and have emotions, you're human too baby."

" I'm good JJ. I'll be fine." She smiled and kissed him on the lips. JJ kissed her back and held her tight. She began kissing him on the neck and removing his clothes. JJ stood up and walked over to the door and locked it. He removed his pants and shoes and climbed in bed.

" I love you JJ." Shyann said.

" I love you more baby."

JJ removed Shyann's underwear and began kissing her inner thighs and worked his was to her vagina. She put her hand behind his head and moaned aloud. He wanted her to feel good and relaxed. He ate her out and she cummed in his mouth, he loved the way she tasted and could eat her out all day if he could. He climbed on top of her and went in bare. She was extremely wet and he couldn't hold his nut and cummed inside of her. He stayed in and continued to pump until he got back hard again.

He flipped her over and gave it to her from the back. Shyann bit down on the pillow to keep from screaming. She moaned and cummed. JJ turned her over and made her get on top and ride. Shyann rode his dick and JJ moaned as he watched her breasts bounce up and down. He grabbed them and pinched her nipples. She laid on his chest and he turned her on her side.

" I'm about to cum." JJ said breathlessly. He gave a few more hard pumps and cummed inside her. They both laid there breathing hard, and feeling good.

" Damn!" Shyann said.

" You good ma?"

" Perfect." She smiled.

" Can I ask you a question?"

" Shoot."

" You ain't got pregnant yet, or my little peoples ain't working?" Shyann began to laugh. "What's funny?"

" Nothing, I'm on birth control, I thought you knew."

" If I knew I wouldn't be asking, now would I?" JJ walked in the bathroom and turned on the shower.

" What are you mad or something?" Shyann walked behind him asking.

" Mad? Naw I'm perfectly fine!"

" Oh, okay! I'm just on some adult shit and if you got a problem address it." Shyann said stepping into his shower water he ran for himself.

" You should've told me that's all." JJ followed her into the shower.

" You should've asked that's all." She said being a smartass. JJ loved Shyann and could never really stay mad at her for longer than 5 minutes.

" I'm being serious. I want a little boy."

" See, that's all you had to do was let me know and I'll handle it. No problem, I'll stop taking my pills tomorrow." Shyann smiled and JJ kissed her.

Shyann was lying, she didn't want any more kids and she wasn't going to stop taking her pills. She thought, if he wanted a baby so bad go knock up the next bitch.

After four weeks her truck was finally ready for pick up. It would've been ready sooner but she had some extra work done to it. She wanted everything bullet proof and she had him paint it white. She had him take off the black 24's and replace them with some white and silver ones she saw and had to have.

Shyann was having second thoughts about reopening the store and moving to Atlanta. She has more than enough money to survive for the rest of her life and if she ever needed more all she had to do was pull her contacts. Shyann was at a very confused stage in her life and for the first time in a long time, couldn't predict her future.

CHAPTER TWENTY-Eight

Life!

" Hey mama." Shyann walked in the kitchen smelling bacon, sausage, grits and eggs being cooked. "I see you're feeling good." Shyann smiled.

" Yeah." Megan replied without making eye contact.

" I'm so tired. I need a vocation."

" People got more issues and problem than you and all you do is complain."

" I do not. Fuck life before it fucks you."

" Watch your mouth child. Get your stuff together and fast. God's coming back and if you ain't right you're getting left behind."

" Mama here you go." She rolled her eyes. "What does that have to do with anything?"

" It has a lot to do with everything, wake up."

" I don't want to hear this shit." Shyann poured a glass of orange juice.

" You should've came to your brother's funeral. . ." Shyann cut her off.

" Mama fuck that, fuck Henry. Leave it up to his dog ass we would've been burring you. He's the one who tried to kill you for some damn insurance money."

" What are you talking about? What insurance money?" Megan walked over to Shyann.

" He tried to kill you to get your insurance money. He so fucking dumb, and I'm so fucking smart I figured that shit out. He tried to switch the policy over to his name, he said fuck you and fuck my kids in so many fucking words. Fuck Henry, I never had a brother!" Megan eyes filled with tears.

" God knows what he's doing child."

" God? God! Where is he now?"

" Baby please don't do this. God is everything and I will not have you stand here disrespecting God. What happened, happened, it was wrong and God fixed it. Do I wish my son were here with me? Yes I do every minute in the day, but he's not, and God isn't the one to blame. Only innocent souls on earth, are babies, Henry was a grown adult.

He did try to hurt me but child, I hear his cries and I forgive him. I forgave him and put it in God's hands. Shyann baby forgive him and move on with your life."

" I will never forgive Henry for what he did. Never!" Shyann walked down the hallway back into her bedroom and closed the door.

" You remember that when you sin and ask God to forgive you." Megan yelled down the hallway.

Megan was doing much better and was ready to move back into her house. She packed her things and Mercedes drove her home. Mercedes was tired of being in the house so she stopped by Chris house. She usually calls before she stopped by, but they had been on good terms so it assumed it would be okay.

She rang the doorbell and Chris yelled, "Coming." Chris came to the door wearing only his boxers. When he saw Mercedes face, he jumped.

" You don't look happy to see me."

" Oh, hey. This is a bad time." Chris said.

" What? What the hell does that mean?"

" Mercedes, look, I'm sorry. Can you please leave?"

" Leave! Chris, I'm so fucking tired of your shit man. What the fuck is going on?" Chris rubbed his head.

" Man." He put his hands over his face. "Porsha upstairs."

" What?" Mercedes eyes filled with tears, she was very emotional due to the pregnancy. "Why is she here? I don't understand, why are you with me if you're still fucking with her?"

" I'm with you because I love you, but you're never here for me."

" I'm not here for you? That's bull shit, so you saying every time one of us feels the other isn't her for the other, go sleep around? NO! You're fucked up Chris and I'll be a fool to have you in my child's life. Fucking fall over a fucking cliff and die because in my world and my babies word you don't fucking exist to us."

" You don't fucking mean that shit." Mercedes walked towards the car and stopped and turned back.

" You think I'm fucking playing, I'll show you." Porsha sat the bottom of the steps listening. Chris wanted to follow behind her but he didn't. He closed the door and saw Porsha sitting there.

" Chris." Porsha said softly.
" Not fucking now."
" Chris I'm pregnant too."
" What? It ain't mines."
" Chris it is and I hope you're not implying I'm a hoe."
" Porsha, you are a fucking hoe. I shouldn't have put my fucking dick in you. This is too fucking much for me."
" What?"
" Bitch let me see a fucking pregnancy test followed by a fucking DNA test. With all that said, get the fuck out my house."
" Bitch? You back on that shit huh? My brothers are going to kick your ass this time I'm not going to save you." Porsha went upstairs to gather her things and Chris went up behind her.
" Look baby, I'm sorry." Chris was scared of her brothers and knew they would fuck him up every time they saw him. "I love you and I'm sorry. You really pregnant?"
" Yes, I just took the test. I have another one if you want me to take it again."
" Naw, I believe you. This is just too much for me. Cedes having twins and now you pregnant. Are you going to keep it?"
" Yes we are!" Porsha looked him in the eyes.

Mercedes drove to the park and walked around the track crying. "God show me the way." She prayed to herself. "Keep me and my kids safe and protect us. God please bless us to make it through and give us strength. God please take the tears and pain away."
Mercedes couldn't understand why he couldn't just be faithful. She was tired and didn't know what to do. She could do all the crying in the world but reality was, it wasn't going to chance anything.

CHAPTER TWENTY-NINE

The things people do!

Bree and Meeka were very close. She couldn't believe what happened to Tish and Meeka and felt she was next. Bree was indeed a hood chick and would murder a nigga in a second, but over the years she became weak and wouldn't harm a fly. When Bree was 16 years old she walked in on her parents having a fight. Bree saw her father, Bill, sock the shit out her mom and sent her flying across the room. Bree grabbed the closest knife to her and stabbed him 7 times in the back.

She really needed a reason to take someone's life, for she know she's not God to determine who should die, so she tries to just chill. But over time people just press the wrong buttons and she looses it completely. Bree got dressed and prepared to hit the stage. She saw Stacy walk in and she knew for a cool minute she and Star was cool. She figured she'd get her high and see if she'll talk.

" What's up?" Bree nodded her head to Stacy.

" Hey, girl! It's mad paper in here tonight. You just getting here?"

" Yup! I'm next on stage but when I get off, I got some shit, meet me in the back."

" Alright."

When Bree got off stage she went to the back and Stacy was standing there smoking a cigarette. Bree approached her and sat at the tables and prepared to lines so they could snort them. Stacy put out her cigarette when she noticed Bree was done and sat next to her.

Bree let Stacy take her line first, then she took hers. Stacy nose began to bleed a little bit.

" Hold your head back Stacy." Stacy held her head back and pinched her nose. "You snorted to hard, bitch your going to kill yourself one day."

" Longs as I die high so I wont feel the pain, I'm good." She laughed.

" Speaking of dieing, I miss Meeka!"

" I know, me too. That bitch stayed with the laughs."

"I wish I knew who killed my nigga. Real shit, I hope they sleep well at night because when I find out who did that, their gonna sleep for the rest of their lives." Bree paused to look at Stacy's expression, but it was nothing there. She assumed she didn't know anything about it so began to talk about Tish.

"First someone attacked Tish and then Meeka. Something ain't right, you feel me?"

"Yeah!" Stacy put her head down and didn't want to make eye contact.

"If you knew who had something to do with that shit, by you being my friend and all, you'd tell me right?" Bree began to put on this said face and fake tears began to roll down her cheeks.

"I'm so sorry for you lost, if I knew anything I would tell you, but I don't!"

"I just thought. . ." Bree paused, knowing the bitch knew something. "I just thought you heard the rumors about Star having something to do with it. I know yall was cool and all. Did she ever mention it to you?" Stacy had completely froze, and Star's voice replayed in her head.

"You don't see shit right?" Star said that night they sat in her truck.

"Naw, I don't know shit." Bree eyes grew bigger and she could no longer hold back. She grabbed Stacy by the neck and chocked her.

"Bitch you wanna play these, I don't know game? Play them with somebody else bitch. You think Star gonna do damage to your ass if you snitch, well I'm going to do worse if you don't!" Bree tightened up on her grib and Stacy struggled to get loose. Stacy took her tumbs and pressed down on both her eyes, Bree felt the pressure on her eyes and felt them about to pop out so she let Stacy's neck go.

"Let me tell you something hoe! If you want to go there with me, we can. I may walk around jolly and shit but bitch come at me sideways again and I swear to father above I will kill you bitch! I said I don't know shit, if I were you I'd leave it at that!"

Bree feared Stacy and felt if she were to go head up with her she just might lose. She judged her by her size and her pretty little smile. Stacy was the type of chick to look out for people who looked out for her, and Star always looked out for her.

" Bitch, it ain't over!" Bree said trying to sound super hard.
" But it will be real soon." Stacy walked into the club and Bree just sat there.

Stacy texted Star and asked her to meet her at Starbucks on LaBrea. At first Star wasn't going to go but Stacy said it was urgent. Star didn't know if she was up to something or not so she had her 9 in back of her jeans. She wore an oversized coat because it was cold out. Stacy didn't know Star painted her truck so she didn't notice her she was already there. Star sat in the car to scope out and see if it was a set up or something. After about 10 minutes she got out the truck and approached Stacy from the back. Stacy jumped when Star touched her on the shoulder.

" Oh shit, you scared me." Stacy stood up to give her a hug.
" My bad, ma! What's good?"
" Shit, what you been up to?"
Shyann wasn't the type to just tell people her business, especially a bitch. She didn't trust'em because all bitches did was talk shit and try to fuck your nigga. "Shit taking care of my kids and Mercedes pregnant so I'm preparing to be a grandmother. What's up with you though?"
" Girl same ole, same ole."
" You still at the club?"
" Yeah I am, that's kind of what I want to talk to you about."
" Oh, word, what's poppin up there?"
" Girl, yo name!"
" Niggas or bitches?"
" You know the niggas ask about yo ass everyday." She smiled. "But this bitch Bree."
" Your home girl? What the fuck that bitch wanna know?"
" She aint my home girl, I almost popped that hoe eyes out last night, the bitch got me fucked up. But anyways, she poppin off at the mouth and shit trying to question me about Tish and Meeka and shit like I'm fucking dumb."

Shyann laughed. "You almost popped the bitch eyes out, that's funny. Look at you getting hood on people. But don't trip off that bitch, I'm going to handle her."

" Naw, I mean that's cool and all but Star I want in. That bitch tried to chock me and shit, she crossed the line. That's why I wanted to meet with you, see you don't work there anymore, so I can be your eyes. We both can get this bitch."

" I usually work alone, when you involve too many people in shit, that's how you get caught."

" Come on Star, I'll play by your rules. I just want in on this bitch!"

" I told you about them grimy bitches before you started fucking with them and your ass didn't listen."

" I know." Stacy shook her head. "What happened with your store?"

" I was remodeling it but I put a hold on it because I may move."

" Yeah, but you can just hire people to run it for you."

" I know, but it's hard for me to trust motha fuckas and I won't be local. I don't know I'll figure it out and work it out soon."

" I know you will, you always handle business."

" Well let me get out of here, I'll hit you up in a few days and tell you what the plan will be."

" Okay, see ya."

Shyann drove to JJ's apartment to chill and smoke a blunt. She began to tell JJ what Stacy told her and how she wanted in. JJ knew Stacy from School but didn't tell Shyann, Stacy didn't know JJ was her dude. So from time to time they'd kick it and hang out. JJ began to get nervous.

" Man, fuck that bitch. Do that shit solo ma." JJ snapped.

" I was thinking that, but Star seem pretty cool though."

" Man that bitch fake."

" You don't even know the chick."

" Right! But, I know how them bitches are who work up there."

" Oh, you do?" Shyann felt offended because she used to work up there as well. "How are the bitches up there?"

" They all hoes and dirty tramps."

" Damn, that's what's up! I guess I'm a hoe and dirty as well huh?"

JJ realized what he said, and backtracked his words. "No ma, not you!"

" Yeah what the fuck ever JJ!"

" Man, it wasn't even like that, you know I wasn't talking about you. I'm just saying don't fuck with that hoe okay?" JJ kissed her on the lips and placed his hand on her face. "I love you."

" Yeah, I love you too JJ." Shyann was too smart for him and his bull shitty ass games. She knew something was up.

Chapter Thirty

Check up.

 TK heard about what went down with Henry and wanted to check up on Shyann to see how she was doing. Shyann was like a sister to him and he would do anything for her as well and he would for Henry. He know the niggs that murdered Henry but was afraid to tell Shyann because he knew how she'd react. Shyann hated Henry right now for what he did to Megan but she didn't want them niggas to murder him.

 TK picked up the phone to dial her number. It went straight to voicemail, so he tried again.

 " Hello." Shyann answered.

 " Hey, Shy it's TK. I'm just calling checking up on you and all. How are you doing?"

 " You know I'm fine, perfect couldn't be better!"

 " Shy it's me, you ain't got to put on a front like things all good, I know they ain't. I'm always here for you if you want to talk. But anyways I know who was behind the murder of your brother. This nigga powerful though."

 " I don't give a fuck, who is he?"

 " Man, I'm not sure if I should tell you."

 " TK, what the fuck you brig it up for? Come on nigga."

 " This nigga named Tyson."

 " Where he at?"

 " Shyann slow down, these niggas is in Jamaica. It ain't shit we can do."

 " Man fuck that! They fucking killed my brother."

 " Shyann Henry stole from them niggas, what did you expect them to do to him? What the hell you gone do? You cant take your heat on the plane and when you get out there you don't even fucking no nobody!"

 " Man TK, fuck that! Fuck them."

 " I know, Shy you gotta chuck this one up as a loss. Look I'm here if you need me, call me anytime. I gotta go."

 " Wait, what city in Jamaica?"

 " Shy don't do whatever your thinkg."

 " I'm not I just want to know."

" Portmore, which is by Kingston. Don't do nothing stupid Shy, they don't play out there. Same thing they did to Henry they'll do to you 10 times worst because you'll be on their grounds. Ain't no calling the police either I heard this nigga Tyson got all that shit on lock."
" Alright, I'll holla at you later. Thanks!"
" Yea, be safe."
Shyann knew everything TK was saying was true and she'd be a fool to go out there and try to murder that nigga and think she'll get out safe. "Fuck" she said to herself aloud. Shyann knew in this situation she couldn't win and decided to just let it go. It hurts her a lot to let things go but she knew she had two kids and two grandkids on the way.

Chris had been calling Mercedes and she hadn't returned any of his calls. He wanted to apologize, but Mercedes really made up in her mind this time that she didn't want anything to do with him. Mercedes was an image of her mom and didn't tolerate bullshit for a long time.
Chris wanted to tell Mercedes face to face about Porsha but couldn't get threw to her. He decided to send her a text message that read: *Cedes, I know you be seeing me calling you! Look I wanted to tell you something, but I can't get threw to you so I'm sending you this text. I'm sorry about everything and I wanted to be the first to tell you Porsha's pregnant, I don't even know if it's mines or not. Look I just thought I'd let you know. Talk to you soon hopefully, love you.*

Mercedes didn't text back, she just simply buried her head into her pillow and cried herself to sleep. Mercedes was very hurt and this was the last time she'd allow a man to hurt her again. She really felt Chris loved and cared for her, and maybe he did somehow. But his actions weren't showing it.
Mercedes began to regret not going through with the abortion. So many things ran through her mind, suddenly a smile appeared on her face. Her babies began to kick, and she didn't feel alone anymore. It was a sign from God reminding her of her blessings.

Her cell phone began to ring and she jumped up. It was an unfamiliar number so she hesitated to answer. She answered and it was a females voice.

" Hello."

" Mercedes?"

" Maybe, who is this?"

" It's Porsha, I'm sorry to bother you, I just wanted to ask you something."

" What the fuck do you want? I heard about your baby, shall I congratulate you?"

" Mercedes, I just called to say I'm sorry and I've decided to get an abortion. I've always pictured being married, living in a big house and then having kids. I haven't told Chris yet, I probably won't either, I just wanted you to know. Look I gotta go."

" Porsha, look, you don't have to get an abortion on my account. Chris and I aren't even together anymore and I don't need him in my life, he can see the kids but that's it."

" No, I'm not doing this because or you or him, I'm doing it for me. I want more in life and Chris can't provide that for me right now."

" Well, I guess. Thanks for telling me."

" No problem, I've realized us women have to stick together at some points. I'll see you around."

Mercedes hung up the phone feeling a bit of relief off her shoulders. She smiled inside, but was unsure why. She didn't want to be with Chris anymore, but she felt having someone's baby was special and you can't just do it with anyone. She wanted to work it out but had too many doubts and heartbreaks. She rubbed her belly and decided to let him go, she concluded she didn't need a man to take care of her because she has God.

CHAPTER Thirty-ONE

Change is needed.

Shyann and Stacy had been watching Bree for several days now and Shyann was ready to make a move on her. Stacy told Bree some dudes were willing to pay 500$ each for 2 hours plus tips, for them to dance at his bachelor party. The greedy little bitch Bree was, said yes of course. Stacy led her to this abundant building in Torrance.

" Girl, this place looks like a dump." Bree said turning her nose up.

" I know, the guy said something about not wanting his wife to find out."

" Shit, they could murder us and no one would ever know."

" Girl please, stop talking stupid. Let's make this paper and go home."

" I feel you that's why I'm here. I just need some drank and I'll be good."

Stacy didn't know that Shyann had JJ and two of his homeboys up there. She wanted it to seem real and wanted to murder Bree herself. All she needed was for Stacy to bring her so she could handle the rest. When JJ saw Stacy walk in, he quickly turned his back. Shyann noted his reaction but didn't say anything because she wanted everything to go smoothly. She stood in the dark, where she was unseen.

Stacy walked over to the guys and smiled when she noticed it was JJ. "I didn't know you were going to be here."

" Okay, so who getting married?" Bree asked.

" Ummm, he is." JJ pointed to his homie. This Tray, and this his best man Cliff." He gave Stacy a look, as to play alone.

" Yeah."

" Why don't yall go get changed while we wait for the other people to come and then we can get started." JJ said.

" Where?" Bree asked.

" Back there, pick a room." Bree headed towards the back and Stacy stood next to JJ for a second.

" What the hell are you doing here?"

" Look, shut up and just follow alone." Shyann came from behind the wall and stood next to JJ and whispered.

" I didn't know you guys knew each other, small world huh? Go get dressed." Stacy turned and walked towards the back.

" So what's up JJ? Yall look pretty close." Shyann asked folding her arms together.
" Ma, we went to School together. She's just an old friend."
" Oh, an old friend and when were you going to tell me you knew her?"
" Man, you trippin', it ain't even like that! Chill."
" Oh, I'm the one trippin'? Fasho' we'll see."
" What the fuck is that suppose to mean? Look they coming go back over there and hide." Shyann shook her head and went back behind the kitchen wall.

" Damn yall sexy!"
" I ain't got all night to wait on yall homies. Press play on that old ass cd player you got and let's get this party started." Bree threw her hands up in the air and began moving her body to New Boys, Jerk.

Tray took full advantage of Bree and put a chair out and asked for a lap dance. He began feeling on her breasts and whispering in her ear. He began kissing her on her neck and with two fingers began rubbing on her pussy. Stacy played alone as well she danced in front of JJ and JJ pushed her away so she could dance with Cliff. Shyann peeked her head from behind the wall and wanted to snatch the bitch up, but she held her cool.

The plan was for Tray to take her into the room and fuck her and Shyann was going to pop that hoe. Bree was easy and would fuck and suck anyone.

" Let's go in the room."
" How much you going to pay me?"
" 3 plus the 5, I'll give you a total of 800$ and when the rest of the fellas get here, you can rack up the tips from them niggas. Come on, what do you say, it's my last night single."

Bree didn't answered, she said yes in body motion. She grabbed his hand and led him into the bedroom. Shyann came back out from the wall and said, "I'm going in there, in 10 minutes. I gotta get home to my kids." She pulled her 38 from her purse and put it on her hip. "Motha fuckas think a bitch dumb and shit!"

" What the fuck are you talking about?" JJ asked.

" Nothing!" She walked over to Stacy, who was dancing on Cliff. "Aye."

" What's up, what you need me to do?"

" Shit, you doing good. What's up with you and JJ? I see how yall looked at each other." Shyann smiled, playing stupid.

" Awww, we used to go to School together, we never had nothing serious."

" Yall ever fucked? He's like a little brother to me, I can hook yall up."

" We did, twice, but that was all, we never dated."

" Oh, that's cool. It was a long time ago?"

" Umm, well the first time yeah, High School. Then the second time was a few months back. Maybe like 5 months ago."

" 5 months?"

" Damn, he didn't tell you he had a girl? Well it's all good, niggas will be niggas, right?" Shyann smiled and walked away.

" JJ tell your homie to bounce."

" What?"

" Tell that nigga to shake, I'll tell Tray myself."

" Look ma, you trippin'."

" You can tell him nicely or I can tell them rudely."

" Man, you on that dumb shit Shy. What brilliant plan do you have up your sleeve huh?"

" I'm ready to go, I have to get to my kids. That's the only plan I'm on because they're all that matters!"

" Cliff shake man. We got it from here my nigga." JJ instructed him to leave and he did just that. "I know you rode with Tray he'll be down in a few minutes."

Stacy come with me. Shyann quietly opened the bedroom door and Bree was on top riding Tray. Tray saw her walk over and she placed her index finger on her lips, which indicated be quiet. Tray began to pump harder and announced he was about to cum. Shyann put her arm around Bree's neck chocking her and pulled her off Tray.

" Tray bounce." JJ stood in the doorway.

" Okay, thanks bitch." He looked at Bree and hopped up and ran past JJ out the front door. Bree fought and struggled to breath, Shyann let her go and she began coughing and trying to catch her breath.

" Bitch! I should've known this was a set up. It's all good though."

" Fuck you, I dislike simple ass bitches and I hate you right now."

" Kiss my ass."

" It would be my pleasure!" Shyann popped her in the head twice. Stacy held her ears and walked to the doorway where JJ stood. Shyann began laughing out loud.

" I hope you feel better Shy?"

" Almost!"

I wanna play a game.

They walked in the living room and Stacy began to put her jeans on. Shyann walked over to her and looked her in the eyes.

" What's up?"

" Remember you asked, what were you going to do? I have the perfect idea." Shyann softly rubbed her pussy with her hand. And kissed her on the lips.

" What you doing ma?" JJ asked.

" Shut up!"

" What's up Star?"

" I want you, that's what's up." Shyann began kissing her on the neck. "Lay down." Stacy didn't want to, but was afraid of what she would do if she said no. And to be honest, Stacy kind of enjoyed the feeling. Shyann removed her shirt and began sucking on her breasts.

JJ stood on the other side of the room biting his lips and quickly grew an hard dick. Shyann undressed herself to just her bra and thong. She began tongue kissing Stacy and Stacy began to kiss her back. Stacy unbuckled her bra and began sucking on her big ass breasts she'd missed seeing bouncing around on stage at work.

" Get on top of me." Shyann whispered in her ear. Stacy got on top and with both there breasts bare pressed against each other turned JJ on even more. "Take off my thong." Stacy was caught up in the moment and felt good, and she did as Shyann asked. "Eat me!"

Stacy began kissing on her stomach and moved down into her inner thighs and began eating her out. Shyann moaned and grabbed her head and made her go deeper. "Yes." She hollered. A woman eats a female pussy better than a man. She knew all the right spots and she stuck her tongue inside her whole and Shyann melted.

" JJ." Shyann called.

" Yeah."

" Come here." JJ walked over with his dick in his hand moaning. "It's some condoms in the room, where Bree body at bring them baby."

" Okay." JJ went to get the condoms and came right back. The sight of Bree lying there dead with blood everywhere was a sight he didn't want to look at for a long time.

" Put it on." JJ put the condom and lay next to Shyann, but Shyann had something else on her mind. "Stacy, ride him." JJ looked at Shyann in shock, he thought he was going to fuck her.

" You sure?"

" Yeah, ride him." Shyann lay there and continued to play with her pussy. Stacy climbed on top of JJ nice and slow and began riding him slowly.

" Oh, yeah!" JJ moaned. Shyann sat up and began sucking Stacy's breasts and took JJ's hand and placed it on her pussy, and he began finger fucking her.

" You like that?" Shyann asked Stacy.

" Hell yeah, give it to me daddy."

" Oh, yeah." JJ moaned.

" JJ, flip her over." JJ flipped Stacy on her back and began giving it to her. JJ thought Shyann was a little freak, but Shyann had something us up her sleeve.

Shyann watched as JJ fucked Stacy with his eyes closed moaning and biting his lips. It was shocking to her because he was fucking Stacy, the same way he fucked her. JJ turned Stacy over and gave it to her doggy style. He pumped harder and harder, sweat rolled down his forehead and Stacy began to moan and holler.

Stacy and JJ both had their eyes closed and didn't see Shyann get up and reach for her heat. They both jumped and opened their eyes when they heard a gun shot. Shyann shot into the ceiling.

" What the fuck?" JJ said.

" You gon' sit here and fuck this bitch like you fuck me?"

" What?" Stacy said. Shyann pointed the gun to her.

" Shut the fuck up, I'm not talking to you. Answer the damn question JJ."

" Man, is that what this is all about?" JJ pulled out of Stacy. "I don't giva a fuck about no bitch."

" Fuck you. You fucked her 5 months ago, is that how you was fucking her then?"

" You trippin', I'm out."

" JJ, I swear to God if you leave I'm going to kill you."

" You ain't gonna do shit, take that gun off that girl she ain't did shit to you."

" Oh, no you taking up for the bitch?"

" Shyann, you need to chill, it's not about taking up for her. You ain't right, that's what it's about. Didn't I tell you I wanted a baby, you still taking them damn pills, I ain't stupid Shy. It's all good though ma, I love you, you don't have to lie to me."

" Oh, is that what this is about? Me taking my pills."

" It's about life and the fact that you have two kids already and a man who loves your ass to death and you still rippin' and running the streets like a little ass kid! And yeah, I fucked her 5 months ago, it didn't mean shit, I'm with your ass everyday.

" You run up to that club and shake your ass and do God only knows what. Ma, get yo shit together and don't worry about what the fuck I do. I said I'm out, and go ahead and think you gon' shoot me or what the fuck ever. I could careless because the only thing that matters to me is having a seed and your selfish grimy ass ain't trying to give a nigga that so shit doesn't really matter if I'm dead or alive."

JJ put his pants on and grabbed his jacket and left. Shyann stood there speechless with a look of shock on her face. Stacy just stood there unsure what to do. Shyann was crazy as hell she thought to herself. She told herself if she made it out this situation she was going to move far away from LA and start over.

" Star, are you okay?"

" I'm fine, I wasn't going to shoot you I was just trying to scare him."

" I'm sorry I didn't know that was your dude, I wouldn't have. ."

" It's cool don't trip, put your clothes on and help me gas this place so we can get out of here please."

" Sure."

Shyann and Stacy poured gasoline in all the bathrooms, bedrooms, on Bree's body and all the walls. She wanted to ensure nothing would trace it back to any of them that were there. She lit a match starting from the back room and threw on on Bree's body then ran out the front door. They hurried downstairs and left.

Sorry!

Shyann got home and checked on the girls and went into her bedroom. She walked into her master bathroom and a hot bubble bath waited for her. JJ stood behind the door so she didn't see him when she entered, he closed the door and she jumped.

" Oh, my gosh. What are you doing?"

" Just relax." JJ began undressing her and helped her into the tub. "I'm sorry ma. I didn't mean the things I said." Shyann covered his mouth with one finger.

" It's okay, if anyone should be apologizing, it should be me. I'm sorry. I love you and I don't want to loose you."

" I love you too ma." JJ loved Shyann with his all and he could never stay mad at her for long.

CHAPTER THIRTY-TWO

A few months later.

Things were perfect Shyann, JJ and the girls couldn't be more happier. They just settled into their new house in Hollywood, Shyann figured if she's going to run her store she needed to be close. Shyann and JJ bought a 6 bedroom, 4 ½ bath home, just north of Highland. She knew someone in the real estate business, so she got him to sale her old home for her. Although the price on their new home was a little pricy, 1.2million was well worth it.

The house had everything they wanted and needed. Pool, Jacuzzi, large front yard, white fenced gate and a huge basement that JJ turned into a studio. The kids had a playroom and a tree house out back, four car garage and a large pool house. It was indeed the dream house Shyann always wanted for her kids.

Shyann wanted Megan to move with them, but grumpy old Megan refused. She explained how much she loved her home and would never leave, but promised to come visit every other weekend. Shyann respected her decision and just to ensure she was okay, Shyann hired a nurse to look after her and check on her daily.

Mercedes hadn't talked to Chris, she didn't tell him they were moving either. She didn't care, she was happy and every time her kids kicked mad her smile more. She was 35 weeks and was ready to bring her blessings in the world. Mercedes was huge, she went from wearing a size 3 to a 10. Her cheeks were fat, ankles were swollen and her body was tired.

Smile!

Shyann walked out on her master bedroom patio in her robe. Inhaling and exhaling the fresh air, she smiled. For the first time in a long time she felt happy and her life seemed complete. She sat in her chair and rolled her last nice fat cush blunt. She decided to stop taking her birth control pills and work on having a son with JJ.

JJ kept his apartment in LA and continued to serve, he wasn't ready to give that lifestyle up yet. He would leave every morning around 9am and come home about 6pm. To him, he felt like it was a job, and I guess it was because he was bringing in a nice income.

" Mama!" Mercedes yelled downstairs from the kitchen. "Mama!" From the tone in her yell she knew something was wrong. Shyann rushed down the flight of stairs to meet Mercedes.
" What?" She said running down the hallway.
" It's time! It's time." Mercedes stood leaning on the counter holding her stomach. Her feet stood still in a puddle of water and it looked like she'd pee'd on herself.
" Oh, my gosh your water broke." Shyann screamed. "Where's your bag, do you have one ready."
" In the room, the pink Adidas duffle bag by my bed. Hurry mama!" Shyann ran into the room and grabbed her bag. She helped Mercedes into the truck and ran back in to put on some sweats and a t-shirt. They drove to Kaiser on Sunset and the doctors took Mercedes into her room.

Mercedes wanted a vaginal delivery, the doctor suggested a Cesarean but Mercedes said no. She had only dilated 3cm and she was in so much pain. Her contraction were bad and she began hollering and screaming. Shyann stood by her side and held her hand.
" Mama, I need something."
" Baby, you can't get an Epidural until 7cm. Your doctor just said that baby, just be strong. I'm going to call Chris, I'll be right back."
" Mama, no! I don't want to see him."
" Mercedes I don't care, he's their father, he deserves to know your in labor. Don't act like that, you about to become a mother. Grow up Mercedes!" Shyann walked into the waiting room and called Chris and told him where they were. She was shocked to know that Mercedes didn't tell him we moved.
She then dialed Megan's number.
" Hey mama, it's time. Mercedes is in labor."
" Oh, thank God. How far along is she?"
" Not far, 3cm. I'm going to call JJ to come get you and bring you up here."
" Okay."

" Okay, I'll call you back Mama." She dialed JJ's cell.

" Hey baby, Mercedes water broke."
" Oh, I'm on the way." JJ said smiling. "How is she going?"
" She's doing well, she's having bad contractions though."
" Can't they give her a pill or something?"
" Yeah, but she has to wait til she dilate 6 more cm. Look babe, can you pick up Lexus from School and my Mom for me before you come, she's at her house."
" Yeah, sure. Do Cedes need anything, or do you need anything? How you feeling?"
" I'm good baby, thanks for asking. We good as of now but I'll hit you if anything changes. Love you."
" Love you more." Shyann pressed end on her cell and smilied. JJ made her so happy.

Shyann went back to check up on Mercedes. She lay there relaxed.
" What he say?" Mercedes asked.
" He's on his way." Shyann sat down on the bed beside her. "Why didn't you tell him we moved? He said he's been looking for you."
" Oh well." Tears began to roll down her face. "Mama I didn't ask for this, I didn't want kids right now. And… and. . he." Shyann wiped her tears away.
" He's just a little boy. You have to teach him how to be a man baby."
" I don't know how. You do, every woman has that power in them to teach."
" Mama, he got Porsha pregnant." Shyann didn't know, so she had a look of surprise on her face. "She called and told me, and then said she was getting an abortion. How could he do me like that Mama, and then he say he love me. That ain't love and if that's how he love, I don't want him loving my kids Mama."
" Baby, he's their father, you can't do that to your kids. He deserves a chance to love them until they decide they don't want his love anymore. Baby, I'm sorry you're going through the things you are so

young, but I been there too. All that matters is keeping smiles on them babies faces, just like I try to do for you and your sister.

" You guys are my world and you guys keep me pushing daily. If Chris wants to be in their lives, let him. It's not a lot of men out here who take care of their kids and you have one who wants to and you won't let him. Cedes that's not fair baby, don't take away something from your kids because you don't want it."

" It's just hard Mama. What do you do when you don't know what to do?"

" You know baby, I'm not perfect and I may not handle situations like I should but I remember I once asked your grandmother that. She answered, pray! Pray and ask God for strength and he'll pull you through and give you the answers you need."

As Shyann talked to Mercedes, she realized she really should be taking her own advice. Chris and Terry walked into the room and Mercedes smiled.

" Hi, Shyann, this is my mom Terry." Chris introduced. "These are for you." Her handed Mercedes a dozen red roses. "I'm sorry." He bent over to give her a hug and kissed her on the forehead.

" I'm glad you're here."

" Me too, how you feel?"

" I'm better now." Chris sat on the bed next to Mereceds and Terry and Shyann decided to go get some coffee.

" So what do you need me to do? I'm here and I'm not going anywhere. Look, you know how it's always been my dream to play football at USC?"

" Yeah, Chris I'm sorry I didn't tell. ." He covered her mouth.

" I got in. I'm going to USC in the fall."

" Oh, that's good!" Mercedes didn't know how to respond. "Chris, I want you to go to School and graduate, just don't forget about your kids, that's all. Can you promise me that?"

" Mercedes we can be a family, Porsha had an abortion, so nothing is standing in the way anymore."

" Chris you're wrong, the fact that you fucked over me twice and got another bitch pregnant, is still standing in the way. I don't want to be with you anymore Chris. I just want to raise our kids and make sure we keep them happy."

" Is that really how you feel? Cedes after all we been through."

" Chris after all you put me through! Yeah I'm sure." Tears rolled down Mercedes face and she let out a scream as a contraction came. Chris didn't know what to do so he ran out and called the doctor.

CHAPTER Thirty-THREE

Almost there.

Mercedes had dilated 7cm and was ready for an Epidural. She could no longer take the pain and signed the papers to have the Epidural Anesthesia. The doctor gave her the Epidural shot into her back and Mercedes felt relieved. She could not longer feel the contractions and she slept peacefully.

" It's time, it's time." The doctor said. Mercedes heard her voice and softly awoke. "I need everyone out please. Megan, Lexus, JJ, Terry, and two of Mercedes friends all exited.

" We're staying." Shyann pulled Chris closer to her. "I'm her mom and he's the father.

"Ok Mercedes", Dr. Adams said. "I need you to relax and breath and when I say push I need you to push. Okay?"

" Yes."

" You two wanna help?" Shyann and Chris both shook their heads yes. "One hold this leg and the other, grab the other." The both moved quickly and followed her instructions. "Mercedes I need you to breath."

Mercedes began to breath and sweat began to roll down her face. She wore her hair in corn rolls and they were pulled back into a bund.

" Okay, I can see the crown of the head, I need you to push." Mercedes pushed as hard as she could. She felt like she was having a vowel movement.

She began to push harder and harder and a few minutes later a little boy came crawling out. Mercedes whole opened so big Chris couldn't bare to look, so he turned his head.

" A boy. Okay one more time, you're doing good, I need you to push." Mercedes began to push and the baby was suppose to come out smooth, but the doctor didn't see the head. "Wait! Stop pushing." We need to perform a c-section."

" What? Why?" The nurse asked.

" The baby is coming out feet first."

" What? How could that be possible?" The nurse questioned.

" What the hell is the baby okay?" Shyann asked.

" Mama what's going on?" Mercedes turned and asked her mom.
" Lord please let everything be okay." Chris said in a low tone.
" Look I need everyone quiet please." The nurse handed her all the tools she needed and the doctor performed the surgery. "The umbilical cord is around the babies neck."

Shyann began to say a prayer within and Chris stood in shock. "Is my baby going to be okay?" Mercedes asked. Dr. Adams didn't reply until about two minutes later.
" Yes, he's fine!" She spanked his butt and he let out a cry.
" Thank you Jesus." Mercedes said smiling. "Can I hold him?"
" Sure."
Mercedes held her baby and kissed him on the forehead. "My little prince."
" So did you decide on names yet?" Chris asked.
" I did! After seeing their faces, I have. The first one is Henry Christopher Malton and the second on is Christian Nate Malton. After my uncle and my dad, I wish they were here." Shyann just smiled.
" I like that!" Chris said.
" Me too!" Mercedes replied.
" They'll be happy to hear the news."

A few minutes later the doctor announced the weight and length of Henry and Christian. Henry was 6lbs 12oz and Christian was 6lbs 2oz born February 27, 2009 at 9:38pm and 9:52pm. The rest of the family came back in along with the God Mama, Jasmine, and Mercedes other close friend Claireese.

Four Days later.
Mercedes and the boys discharged and went home. She was happy, although her body was tired she laughed and cuddled with her kids all day long. When they cried in the middle of the night Mercedes got up with a smile and fed them and changed them. Chris would come over everyday and help with the kids. Mercedes felt all this would change once he went to School, but she kept her comments to herself.

Shyann helped her as well and Lexus would try. She tried to help change Henry and had powder everywhere. Mercedes wanted to get made, but when she noticed she looked like a snowman, couldn't do anything but laugh. Mercedes was happy, and her babies allowed her to love and be loved.

JJ wanted to do something special for Shyann's 32nd birthday, and wanted it to be a surprise. It was just a few weeks away and if he wanted it to be nice he had to act immediately. Her birthday was on arch 28th which just happened to fall on a Saturday. JJ made a few phone call and hired a party planner and it seem everything else was easy from there.

CHAPTER THIRTY-FOUR

Rise and Shine!

JJ awoke Shyann with soft kisses on her neck. She smiled when she opened her eyes.

" Good morning beautiful, Happy Birthday." Shyann sat up.

" Thanks baby."

" Close your eyes." JJ said.

" For what baby?"

" Just do it baby." Shyann closed her eyes. JJ reached under the bed and removed 3 small boxes and 2dozen roses and placed them on the bed. "Open!"

" What is this?" Shyann said smiling.

" I love you baby, first I have 2dozen roses. Here open this one." JJ handed her on of the boxes. Shyann opened the small box and it was a pair of 24k gold diamond earrings.

" Oh, my gosh. I love them baby, thank you!" She gave him a big hug.

" Okay, okay, wait it's more. Open this one!" He handed her another box. Shyann opened the box and it was a 24k gold neckless with a heart charm with diamonds in it.

" Baby you shouldn't have. Thank you I love it."

" Okay last one, here." She took the last box and opened it. It was a 24k gold bracelet with diamonds all around it.

" Thank you so much baby." She kissed him. Shyann was very greatful but she thought a ring was in one of the boxes, so she was a little disappointed.

She felt if a nigga really loved you and wanted to be with you he wouldn't hesitate to lock you down. She kind of felt they were moving to fast anyways when they bought the house together. But JJ ensured her if anything happened to them she could keep the house.

" I want to take you out to dinner at 9pm so be ready, I'll be back later. Love you."

" Okay, love you too."

Shyann took a shower and got dressed. Mercedes and Lexus surprised her with a home made German chocolate cake, Shyann's favorite.

" Surprise." Lexus screamed as Shyann walked into the kitchen to pour a glass of arrange juice.

" Oh, you scared me." Mercedes came from the dining room holding the cake in her hands.

" Happy birthday mama."

" Thanks guys." Shyann smiled. "Where's the babies?"

" Sleep, so what did JJ get you?" Mercedes placed the cake on the counter and took out three plated from the cabinet.

" Some jewelry."

" It wasn't just some jewelry Lexus, it was diamonds." Mercedes said as she took a knife out the drawer and handed it to Shyann.

" Diamonds, wow, are they pretty?" Lexus asked.

" Their gorgeous! How do you guys feel about JJ?" Shyann replied.

" I love him." Lexus said.

" Yeah, he real cool mama. Why you asking?" Mercedes answered.

" I'm just asking." Shyann cut three pieces of cake and handed the girls a plate. "Now, normally I wouldn't let yall have cake this early, but since my favorite girls made this specially for me, Happy Birthday to me." They all began to laugh. Shyann took a fork full and put it in her mouth. "Taste really good too."

" Were glad you like it mama." Mercedes said.

" Umm, how did you know JJ bought me diamonds Cedes?" Shyann asked.

" He asked me help him puck them out. I thought you would like them."

" I do, don't get me wrong."

" I picked out a diamond ring but he said the time wasn't right. But there was this gold ring, it has a big diamond in it, he kept staring at it."

" Oh, ok. Well I'm going shopping. Who wants to come?"

Shyann analyzed her situation and realized that she in fact did want to get married. She wanted to sit down and talk to JJ about it, but didn't want him to feel pressured. She really loved JJ and felt he was the one. She truly cared about him and saw a future.

Shyann was Shirley Temple curling her hair and Mercedes walked in holding Christian. She just watched her mother while feeding Christian his bottle.

" Hey." Shyann turned towards Mercedes.

" Hey, where you going?"

" Dang, you sound like the mother!" Shyann smiled. "JJ taking me out for dinner."

" Oh, where?"

" I don't know. What's up with all the questions?"

" Nothing just asking. You wearing this?" She pointed to a short Champaign dress lying on her bed.

" Yeah, you don't like it?"

" Yes, its really cute. Back out and all, when I loose my weight I wanna try it on."

" Girl, this dress is too grown for you. And where you going to wear it at?"

" I don't know, I just wanna look beautiful like you."

" So what you trying to say I make ugly babies?" They both laughed.

" No mama, never mind. I hope you have a good time."

" Me too, I just want a peaceful night, drama free. Ya know?"

" I know exactly how you feel, that's how I feel about my life. Mama can I ask you a question?"

" Shoot."

" How many chances are you suppose to give someone you love?"

Shyann put her curls down and turned to look at her daughter. "Cedes, there's no limit when it comes to love. God gives us chance after chance to get our shit together and he still loves us."

" I know, I mean human beings. It's easy for God because he was born to love us."

" You and your sister drive me crazy at times, and I never stop loving you guys."

" Why did you stop loving daddy?"

" Your father stopped loving me and thought I was suppose to put up with his bullshit day in and day out. I love your father, over years we grew apart and not together." Her eyes filled with tears. "If I could

go back in time and redo it all, I would. But things happen for a reason and I'm happy right now."
" I'm saying, you and daddy was like white on rice, I remember you guys was happy too."
" Was baby, was! What you asking all these questions?"
" Because I want someone to love me like daddy loves you. Every time I talk to him, you're always the topic of the conversation. No matter what we're talking about he finds a way to tie you with it and we end up talking about you." Shyann began laughing.
" What?"
" I'm serious mama, I wanna be loved."
" Cedes, you are loved! I love you, your father loves you, Lexus loves you, JJ loves you as well and most importantly them babies love you. You're going to have to teach them how to love and it starts by being an example. What ever they see you do and how you allow a man to treat you is how they're going to treat women. Remember that."
" I guess that is true, I just want." Mercedes paused. "Never mind."
" Want what?"
" Nothing."
" Want Chris to love you?"
" Maybe."
" Mercedes Chris loves you. ."
" No he don't!" She cut her off.
" He does baby, he loves you. He's just not loving you the way you want to be long. Look baby you're about to be 17, you have plenty of time to experience love."
" Yeah, how much time does a person have when their steady pushing the other person away. Thanks for the chat, have a good night." Mercedes replied smart and started towards the door with Christian.
" Hey!" Mercedes stopped. "I love you."
" I love you too mother!" Mercedes smiled and headed down the hallway towards her room.

A night to remember!

JJ stood in front of a white Hummer limo as Shyann opened the front door.

" Why are you ringing the doorbell?" Shyann said looking beautiful as ever. "What is this baby?"

" Wow! Give me a spin." Shyann turned slowly around in her 4 inch gold heels. She wore her jewelry JJ bought for her and smelled lovely, wearing Sean John Unforgivable for woman. "I am indeed blessed! You look amazing, I wanna say fuck tonight and lets make love all night."

" JJ shut up." Shyann began to laugh. "I look good huh?"

" Hell, good don't describe the way you look baby."

" Thank you."

CHAPTER Thirty-FIVE

Never happy for long!

Shyann and JJ pulled up to club Ivar In Hollywood. The line was around the corner and everyone was dressed to impress and looking good. Shyann was the hottest bitch walking the streets of LA and was well known. People would pay anything just to be in the same room as her. Word got around town and everyone was there. Stacy even heard about it and she moved to San Diego.

" What's this?" Shyann rolled down her window. JJ didn't reply.

" Aye driver stop at the front." The driver nodded and did as he was asked. He opened the door for them to get out everyone stopped and stared.

" Oh, my gosh is this party for me?"

" Yup! I got the hottest spot in Hollywood, the best DJ and I walking with the finest female in town." JJ said so big headedly.

" Awww, thanks babe!" She gave him a kiss and they walked in. Music was bumping loud as Jay Z and Alicia Keys was blasting through the speakers.

" In New York. ." Shyann began to sing along. JJ walked her over to their VIP area. A few of their homeboys came over to join them and wished Shyann a Happy Birthday. JJ made sure to have her favorite drink, Patron, of course.

" Let's get these shots started." Shyann yelled.

Shyann was feeling herself and worked her way to the dance floor with JJ. She hadn't been to the club since JJ's party. She grind and moved her hips to the music and JJ kept the shots coming. He handed her the blunt.

" I'm cool baby."

" What?"

" I'm good baby." She said continuing to dance on him. "I'd thought I'd stop if were going to work on this baby." Shyann smiled.

" Oh, is that right?" JJ pulled her closer. "But you drinking baby."

" I know, this my last night drinking, besides I can piss this shit out later, that shit gonna be in my system for a while." She said pointing to the blunt.

"Okay. Cool ma, that's what up! I'll be right back."

"Where you going?"

"Over here for a minute and see if these niggas TK'em wanna hit this shit."

"Ok, I'll be right here grooving." Shyann kept dancing. Stacy spotted her from across the room and came by to say hi.

"What's up ma? Happy birthday." Stacy gave her a hug. Shyann wasn't really feeling the hoe like that, but felt bad for what she did to her that night in the apartments.

"Hey, I'm glad you made it. How's San Diego?"

"It's real cool, the money is bomb. I'm racking like 2g's a night. Them niggas love black women. What you been up to?"

"Nothin, Cedes had her baby and I reopened my store, JJ and I bought a house together. Were doing good."

"Look ma, sorry about what happened between JJ and I."

"Stacy shut up and dance. The past is the past." Shyann pulled Stacy closer towards her and began dancing. A guy walked by and bumped Shyann and didn't say excuse me.

"Excuse you fucker!" Shyann snapped.

"What?" The guy turned around and said.

"Your bitch ass bumped me fucker, say excuse me."

"Bitch fuck you." Shyann walked closer to him.

"I got your bitch." Shyann kneed him in the balls and he slapped the shit out of her. Shyann spit on him the upper cut him with her right fist followed by the left and that nigga feel to the fucking floor. JJ saw and flew over there fast as hell.

"What the fuck ma?" JJ snapped.

"This bitch ass nigga got me fucked up. It's my fucking birthday, I'm finna party like a fucking rock star." The security came over and picked the dude up off the floor.

"Fucking bitch, I'm from New York, Harlem bitch!"

"Nigga fuck you, I'm from the streets of LA, Crenshaw bitch!" JJ gave that nigga one hit that put that nigga straight to sleep. Shyann began laughing.

195

" Get this nigga out of here." JJ requested. "Ma you need to chill." Shyann rolled her eyes.

" Nigga, miss me." She walked away and began dancing again. Everyone in the club just looked and a few seconds later began dancing again.

" Get the fuck out!" The security officer told the dude, throwing him onto the curb.

" That bitch gon' die. Tell her Marcus said that shit." He walked towards his car.

" Yeah, yeah. You're drunk, go home."

Shyann and Stacy went back to the VIP area and had shots of Patron. JJ was embarrassed with how Shyann acted. But he knew that was the type of chick she was, she didn't need a nigga for shit. And she made sure people knew that, but JJ wanted to feel needed. He wanted to feel like he was the man and he had to protect his woman.

" Dang ma, it's your birthday don't be getting your nails dirty." TK whispered in her ear in a playful tone.

" I know, you already know how I am though, I don't like people fucking with me."

" I know but you got all of us here with you, we got you if you let us. Chill, next time just holla and we'll handle it fo' ya ma. Alright?"

" Alright." TK has always been there for her so she respected him and what he had to say. With Henry gone, TK was like the only brother she had right now. She wondered what the girls were doing so she sent Mercedes a text saying, hey hope you guys are okay, I'll be home shortly. Make sure the alarm is set. Love u.

A few seconds later Mercedes sent one back replying, we love you too and we're good. Chris came over to keep us company. Hope your having fun, see you soon. Closed with a smiley face.

Shyann read the text and a smile appeared over her face and at that moment all she wanted to do was go home to her kids. She walked over to where JJ was standing with some friends.

" Hey."

" Hey ma, you cooled off?" JJ asked.

" Yeah, I'm good. I'm ready to go." JJ looked down at his watch.

" It's not even midnight, it's barely 11:30."

" I don't care, I'm ready to go. Look, don't trip I'm finna bounce."

" All these people are here for you ma, and you just gonna leave?"

" I don't know half these people in here and their not her fo' me, their here to see what's up and go back and run their mouths."

" So you really finna act Hollywood ma, like your better than people now?"

" It's not about acting Hollywood. I don't give a fuck about nobody in here but you and TK so fuck these people. I'm out!" Shyann headed for the front door. JJ wanted to go after her but he had had enough of her damn attitude. She signaled the limo driver to come from across the street and he flashed his light, indicating ok. She stood with her hands folded waiting. Something told her to walk back into the club but she didn't and she was upset with JJ not leaving as well. "I just wanna go home." She said in a low tone to herself.

What matter most?

" Bitch!" A voice yelled from a dark colored vehicle stopped in the middle of the street. Shyann being the badass chick she is, with her I don't give a fuck attitude walked towards the car.

" Who you calling a bitch?" Shyann saw him reach over to the passenger's seat and she knew something was about to go down. She didn't fear anything and stood there boldly waiting for whatever he had in store for her. All the things Shyann had done in her past, she knew eventually her time would come, that's why she lived everyday like it was her last and shitted on anybody who crossed her path wrongfully.

Marcus pulled out a crone 40glock and got off with all 17 shots. Shyann turned and tried to run back in the club. Shyann normally carries her heat everywhere she goes, but tonight she was bare and pissed. The crowd screamed as shells hit the ground. She almost made it to the door, Shyann fell face down with blood flowing everywhere. The smell of burnt tires filled the air as Marcus pulled off.

JJ heard guns shots and thought of Shyann. He ran outside but it was too late. Shyann had been hit 3 times in the chest, once in the shoulder, and once in the leg. JJ ran into the middle of the street and began busting at the car. TK and his crew hopped in their cars and followed him. JJ eyes began to fill with water as he stared at Shyann's body, the security officer called 911.

" Fuck man!" JJ kneeled down beside Shyann and picked her up as if he was holding a baby. "It's okay, ma. You're going to be okay baby."

" Tell my kids I love them and I love you." Shyann said breathlessly.

" No baby, when you get home, you can tell them. You're going to be alright, just hold on. Where the fuck is the ambulance at? Fuck!" Everyone just stood outside in tears and shock. Stacy called the police again.

" 911 is this an emergency?" The operator asked.

" Yeah, I need an ambulance, someone's been shot." Stacy said crying.

" Who mam? I need you to calm down. Did you see the shooters?"

" My friend, Star, I mean, Shyann. I didn't see the shooter but the security may know who he is. Look bitch can you stop asking all these damn questions and send someone."

" Look mam, I know you're upset but I have to ask these questions an officer is on the way." Stacy hung the phone up while two officers pulled up, followed by an ambulance. The officer pulled out his pad and pen.

" Man you see me standing here and blood is everywhere and your bitch ass pull out a fucking pad and pen. Man, fuck you." JJ walked passed the officers towards the ambulance truck and an EMT came running towards him.

" She's loosing a lot of blood. We have to get her to the hospital quickly." They took Shyann's body and put her into the truck. JJ stayed by her side the whole ride.

"Hold on baby. Hold on. He needs to drive faster." JJ snapped at the EMT lady.

"Look sir, we're doing everything we can, please calm down."

"I'm sorry, this is my baby right here and I don't know what I'd do without here."

"I understand." Shyann was barely breathing, JJ just held her hand tight and prayed to himself.

"Please pull through baby. Please." He whispered. Shyann closed her eyes and let out a deep breath.

"Tell my kids I love them please." JJ began crying.

"Just hold on, we're almost there. I'm going to get them to get you a blood transfusion and you're going to be okay baby. I promise, just hang on a little bit longer." JJ turned to the EMT. "Is she going to be okay?"

"I don't know sir." She replied then put her head down.

TK and his boys caught up with that nigga Marcus and killed that nigga. He begged and pleaded for mercy and TK blew his fucking brains out. TK couldn't believe this nigga thought he was going to get away with what he had done. Even though Marcus was dead, that wasn't going to save Shyann and bring her back.

Shyann passed away 20 minutes after she reached the hospital. JJ stood on the rooftop of Kaiser and was about to jump. Shyann was the world to him and he felt he had no reason to live. He began to sob and couldn't handle the pain. The image of Shyann's smile replayed in his mind of when he gave her the jewelry earlier that morning. He felt like it was his fault, maybe if he hadn't had thrown her the party she'd still be here. So many thoughts ran through his mind.

Then he saw two little boys running pass him, it was Henry and Christian. A smile appeared on his face then he began crying again. He knew he had to be there for Mercedes, Lexus and the twins. Megan could take care of them but they needed a father figure. Megan was going through enough herself, and loosing her only two kids to the streets in less than 6 months was enough.

All Shyann wanted to do was go home to her kids and had she stayed in the club or maybe if JJ walked her out she'd still be here. All that ever mattered most to her was her kids. And now that doesn't matter at all because she's no longer here. So sometimes what matters most doesn't matter at all, because when you die it's not much you can take with you.

BONUS:

Featuring poems from *Pain, Wrong turn!*

Don't love me unfair

You once said, you were crazy about me!
We'll be "crazy about me" & show you care
I didn't have intentions of you loving me unfair
I'm not perfect nor or you
We're going to have ups and downs
 that's what people in love do!
So why would you want to take that away?
Do you not hear the emotions when I say,
 I love you, I need you or I wish you were here?
Baby forgive me and don't love me unfair
They say follow your heart
But sometimes your heart can tear you apart
Follow your feet and I'll meet you halfway
Our perfect ending will come soon one day
Until then let's try our hardest to make it through
I hurt you, true! But baby you hurt me too.
Please don't let go
I'm giving my all and believe we can grow
From the bad to the good
I'll always remain your chick from the hood.
So baby please don't love me unfair
Just give me one more chance to truly show I care.

What Matters Most

Sometimes what matters most doesn't matter at all,
Because when your back is against the wall,
How hard could you possibly fall?
How easy could it be for you to bounce back?
How hard is it for you to let go and don't look back?
I hear people complain and say they want to live a stress free life,
Why complain when you're the one rolling the dice?
You determine if you win or lose!
But really, who looses when you didn't choose?
Simply give your heart and soul in everything you do!
So I must ask you,
What matters most?
I overhear silence covering the room as if your souls are ghost,
You can have the whole world in your hands,
But if you plan on going to heaven they will not get in.
You cry on that bathroom floor seconds from being dead,
Hoping and praying someone walks in with words unsaid,
Because you feel everything in your life has fallen apart,
And believe, what's more apart than living without a heart?
So what matters most when you're ready to take your life?
Now what should matter is, getting your hands on them dice,
And roll them like you never rolled them before,
Then trust in God and he'll open another door!
Are you trying to escape the pain or is the pain trying to escape you?
So what matters most? Nothing at all, things rise and things fall!

BONUS:

Featuring two chapters from *A Cry For Help!*

CHAPTER 1

It seems like every little thing I do or say he ready to knock me upside my head. Last night he hit me so hard I still can feel the pain. I love him and he said he's going to get help before it's to late. I wanted to ask, to late for what, but he would of just hit me again and told me not to ask him any questions. Everyone tells me I should leave him, but I cant he makes me happy and he's the only one that cares about me and I love him too much.

"Tracey, Come here." Brain called.
"Yeah."
"Girl don't, yeah me, say yes."
"Yes."
"What you in there doing? Fix me something to eat and clean up the bathroom, I had a little problem in there."
"I was folding up some clothes. What do you want to eat?"
"Girl it doesn't matter, just fix me something and stop asking me questions."

I really don't feel like doing anything, but I can't tell him that. I went in the kitchen and took out some chicken, cabbage and potatoes and sat it on the counter. Then I went in the bathroom to look at what mess he was talking about. Before I could get to the door a bad odor took my breath away. I opened the door and shit was everywhere, I mean everywhere. It was all around the toilet, cabinets, shower curtain, walls and floor. I threw up right there on the floor I couldn't even throw up in the toilet if I wanted to because it was over flowed. It took me an hour to clean that shit up. Brain went in there and went to sleep. I cooked his meal for him and served it to him in bed. He took the plate and threw it into the wall.

"What's that for?" I said, standing with my mouth open in shock!
He said, "Didn't I tell you I was hungry two hours ago?"
"Yes, and you also told me to clean the restroom."
"Are you talking back to me?"
"No."
"Go in there and fix me another plate, then… clean up this mess. Can you follow those directions?"

"Yes."

I only cooked enough for the both of us, so if I fix him another plate I'm not going to have anything to eat. He doesn't care though, that's just how he is and I've learned to deal with it after three years. I took him his plate and cleaned the food off the floor and wall. By the time I was done cleaning it all up he was done with his dinner so I took his plate and put it in the kitchen. He didn't say thank you, or anything like that but I know he means it. My stomach started to growl. I was tired I didn't feel like cooking anything else so I ate a sandwich. I just wanted to lie down so I took a shower and went to bed.

Ring! Ring! Ring!
It had to be about three a.m. and the phone is ringing. I take it Brain didn't hear it because he would of answered it, so I grabbed it.

"Hello", no one answers. "I said hello." I said.
"Can I speak to Brain?" A girl said.
"Who is this?" I said.
"Is this Tracey? Girl put Brian on the phone."
" Who is this?"
"Bitch, tell Brian to call KayKay when he get a chance."
"I ain't relaying no messages to my man from a bitch. Don't call our house any more unless you want problems."
"That's on you if you don't relay this message, because I'm sure he's relaying his messages to you." *laughs and hands up the phone!*

I tap Brain and tell him to wake up. He's in a deep sleep and can't hear me. So I get up and turn on the light and stand over him and scream and shout for him to hear me. I saw the cover lift up and his hand came flying across the right side of my face. He slapped me.

"What do you want? Don't you see me sleep? It better be important!"

I didn't say anything because by this time I could see he was very angry so I backed up away from the bed and held my face.

"You're going to answer me." Brain said.
"KayKay called. I just wanted to know who she was." I said.

" Did you wake me up to ask me about a damn phone call? What the hell is your problem girl? I'm getting tired of you being all in my business."

I didn't say anything, because I didn't know if he was just saying that or if he wanted a response.

"You don't hear me talking to you Tracey?" Brain said.
"Yes. I just wanted to know."
" I'm getting tired of you, I really am. She is just a friend."

I didn't believe him but what could I do call him a liar. That would of made things worst. I lay down beside him and he grabs me and begins kissing me on my neck and running his hands across my body. It felt so good and I wasn't mad anymore because he may hurt physically but emotionally he takes care of me. He started taking off my clothes and kissing my body he went down to kiss me in between my legs. It felt so good I wanted to stay in this moment forever. Then he climbed on top of me and gave it to me nice and slow and asked me if I liked it. I shooked my head yes.

Brain spread my legs open wider and started going faster. I grabbed his back and held him tight he pushed my arms off him and went faster and harder. It felt like he was tearing my pussy walls apart. Harder and harder, I begged him to slow down because he was hurting me. He was sweating like a dog, I began screaming and hollering, *Stop! Please! That's enough!* But he kept going anyways, faster and faster. I began to cry, that's how bad the pain was. I felt him about to cum and he pulled out and nutted on my stomach.

"You like that, huh." Brain said. "I know I did."

I didn't say anything, he got a towel and wiped the nut off my stomach and kissed me on the forehead and put the covers on me. I rolled over and feel asleep.

The next morning I woke up at about ten a.m. Brain usually wakes me up to fix his lunch at eight but I guess he wanted me to rest. Brain works at the bank in Highland he's the President but he does a lot of his work on the streets. We stay in the city of Applelynn he runs these streets and everyone respects him and even if they don't they pretend like they do. I'm not really sure exact what it is he does but I know it has to do with drugs. I have to get ready for school my class starts at eleven and I'm going to be late.

I go to Applelynn University this is my third year. It's cool, its not High School though. In High School I was most popular and captain of the cheerleading team. I been out of school for three years. I was an honor student with A's and B's and I graduated with an overall g.p.a. of 3.96.

I got a job for the summer at the Gap, that's where I met Brain he was in there shopping with his daughter, Alicia, she's 13, she's so pretty. Alicia's mom is Mexican and Black so she's mixed with long pretty hair and hazel eyes. Brain asked to take me out and I said yes. He asked how old I was and why was such a pretty thing like me was working. I told him I just turned 18 last month and I saving up money to buy a car. Then he wrote his name and number down and left.

Now three years later were living together and he bought me a Lexus and made me quit my first and only job the second week of dating. Brain been there for me every since. He's all I know and all I want to know. The only difference is our age he's 36 and I'm 21 now. But I've learned age is just numbers.

CHAPTER 2

I entered the class and everyone is looking at me funny. I know I'm late but damn it's only 15 minutes. I say, "*What?* ", real loud.

" Take your seat Ms. Williams". The professor says.

I sat down next to Maria, one of my Hispanic home girls in the class.

"What's up girl?" Maria says.
"Nothing girl, these people up in here about to get slapped one by one."
"What happen to you?"
"What?"
"Your face girl."

I'm sitting there thinking to myself oh yeah, Brain did hit me last night. Damn that's why these people laughing at me. I was rushing this morning and I didn't put on my make up. Everyone know who I talk to and they already know what he about but I just play dumb because I'm embarrassed.

"I got into it with some girl yesterday that hit my car." She looked at me as if she knew I was lying, but I didn't care.
"Yeah girl, I hope you alright. If you ever need anything call me."

She took a piece of paper out her folder and wrote her number down on it and put it on my desk.
" Your not alone, and there's always going to be someone out there who love you and who's thinking about you." She said.
" Thanks, but I'm fine." I took out my notebook and began writing down the notes from the professor.

After class the professor stopped me and asked if he could talk to me for a minute about my grade. I shook my head yeah and walked over to his desk.
" Yes." I said.
" I'm not trying to be in your business...", the professor said and I rudely cut him off.
" Then don't."

"I'm just concerned about you. Is everything okay?"

"Just fine."

"Do you need any help in your personal life or anything like that? Because I'm here to help you Ms. Williams."

Slight laugh. "I thought you wanted to talk to me about my grade not my personal life. Are you trying to hit on me or something, because if you are I have all rights to take proper action because I'm feeling a little harassed right now."

"No Ms. Williams, it's not like that. I apologize. You had an A but you failed the last test and it dropped you down to a C. I wanted to know if you were interested in taking it over. I'm having one day of make up work next week on Tuesday at 9a.m. if you want to take it over please be here."

"That's all?"

"Yes Ms. Williams, that'll be all. Have a good day."

"Thank you."

I got one more class so let me go to the restroom and put on my make up so I won't have to hear anyone else mouth. I walk down the hallway and as I'm enter the restroom I over hear Brain's name. I wasn't tripping because there's a million Brains, but it made me think about him. I pushed the door open and put my bag on the counter and took out my make up bag. The two girls that I overheard talking looked at me and laughed.

I said, "What's funny."

"Oh nothing." One of the girls said, grabbing the other on and exiting the restroom giggling.

I finished my make up and was looking brand new. I decided to call Brain to see what was going on with him. *Ring! Ring!*

"Yeah." Brain answered.

"Hey baby, I'm at school, I was just thinking about you."

"Oh that's good, how's your day?"

"Fine and yours?"

"Good Trace."

"How about we go out for dinner tonight, sounds good?"

"Great I'll be home by seven, then we can go. Okay I have to go I'll see you later Trace."

Brain always gets the last words, that's just how he is. Sometimes he can be as sweet as I don't know what and I love him for that. I'm just going to check in this class and turn in my homework so I can go to the mall and nail shop. I want to look my best for Brain because he likes to see me dressed and smelling good.

I pull up at the nail shop and see my girl Krystal. Krystal and I were best friends in High School. She went to Arizona to stay with her grandmother and we slowly lost contact with each other.

" Tracey." Krystal says, as she runs and gives me a hug. " I missed you Trace, why you ain't called nobody."
" Hey girl, how are you?" I said smiling.
" I'm fine. This Lexus you."
" Yes."
" I see you doing good mommy. You getting your nails and feet done?"
" Yes, what about you?'
" Yeah, so come on so we can talk. You know you still my best friend Trace."
" Yeah girl, I know."

We enter the nail shop and they ask us want we need, we tell them and they give us a seat next to each other. Kris and I talked about High School and we were just laughing and joking. She asks me who am I with and how's my relationship going.
Kris doesn't know about Brian so from what I told her she thinks he's perfect. She told me she has two kids and a boy two and a girl four months and that they're the best thing that ever happen to her.

She told me how her ex started beating her and she had to leave him that's why she's back out her because she couldn't deal with it anymore. I sat there with a guilty conscious. I didn't say anything because Kris is a good friend but she likes to talk and I mean talk. She's the type that doesn't listen to well, so she'll go back and tell a totally different story. So I didn't tell her big mouth anything. Our hands and feet were done and I told Kris not to worry about it I'll pay.

"Girl I got it, don't trip." Krystal said.

"Kris it's nothing." I handed the lady a one hundred dollar bill the total was eighty-four dollars. "Keep the change sweetie." I told the Chinese lady.

I glanced over to look at Krystal and she stood with her mouth open.

"Are you okay?" I said.

" Are you?"

" Yes why, what happened Kris?"

" You just trying to show off and shit like you just all that. Girl I remember when you ain't had a dime to your name and didn't even have nothing to eat. Now look at you, you think you the queen or something rolling up in your Lexus and wearing all this fine jewelry and stuff pulling out credit cards and hundred dollar bills and shit. I remember when your crack headed ass mama wouldn't even buy you shoes for school because her high was more important, who ended up buying them, my mama. Girl you haven't went over there checked up on her or nothing like that"…..

I cut her off. "Girl I don't want to hear that."

She grabbed me back and said, "you need to hear it."

She pulled me outside of the shop next to my car. " Tracey, my mom took you in, she did as much for me as she did for you. You never once went over there and seen how she was doing. Tracey I ask my mom about you everyday, she say word on the street is you laid up with some old man and he hitting you and shit. Tracey you don't have to put up with that. My mom said your mom put you out, you know you could have went to stay with my mom. Tracey if he has to hit you to get his point across because you make him that mad, then maybe you don't need to be with him. Girl you pretty and smart, let him go."

I didn't say anything because everything she was saying was true and I know that but he's making a huge difference in my life right now and no one understands that but me. "I have to go Kris." I said.

" That's the Tracey I know always running away from her problems, all the time but she want run away from getting beat every night."

" Yeah, that's me and so what. You always had your family there for you and you have one of the best mom's. What do I have nothing, nobody. I sometimes don't even have myself. When I'm alone and scared who can I talk to or who can I ask for help? NOBODY! Nobody at all, I'm alone and even if I wanted to leave, where would I go? Huh, tell me back with my mom, so she can steal from me and have people running in and out of the house all day and night and have me raped just to get a rock." I started breaking down crying.

    Krystal came closer to me and embraced me with a hug and told me it's okay and that she's sorry, she wasn't trying to hurt me but she taught I would have since enough to know I deserve better. Every thing she said was true and was what I needed to hear from someone who cared about me.

    " Look at me Tracey, I love you girl and I'm going to help you, but only if you want it." Krystal said.
    " Thanks." I said.

    We exchanged numbers and I didn't feel like going to the mall anymore so I just went to the house and picked out a dress I never wore from the closet. I was thinking about what Krystal was saying to me and started thinking about everything. I don't feel like doing anything now because my minds just wondering. It's about five and Brain and I are suppose to go out at seven I don't feel like going, but I can't tell him that. He'll get mad or upset because he changed his plans so we could go out. I got dressed a Brain came in at 5:30 and told me he'll be ready in a couple of minutes.

    I wore this red tight dress that stopped at my thighs I had in the closet because after talking to Krystal I didn't feel like going to the mall. I had on some silver pumps and a little silver purse I couldn't fit anything in but my lipstick. Brain came out, looking good as usual. He was dressed in a black suit with a red tie and red shoes. I wanted to say let's forget about dinner and get to the desert.

"You look very nice." Brain said.
"And so do you." I said.

    He took my hand and led me to the door and opened it for me. Then we got in his cherry red 745 on 22's and drove off. We went to this Italian restaurant and dinned. After we ate he told me to drive because he had a little too much to drink. We got home and went inside a fell straight asleep.

MORE INFO ABOUT THE AUTHOR VISIT Keishababy.com